the ultimate book for pasta lovers
truly madly pasta

Rizzoli
NEW YORK

truly

madly

Ursula Ferrigno   **photography by Peter Cassidy**

pasta

To Richard, my rock and roots, for all you do. I love your cooking too.

1 le fondamenta
basics page 6

2 zuppe e
minestre
soups page 16

5 leggero e sano
light & healthy page 82

First published in the United States of America in 2003 by **UNIVERSE PUBLISHING**, a Division of **Rizzoli International Publications**, Inc. 300 Park Avenue South, New York, NY 10010

First published in 2003 by **Quadrille Publishing Limited** Alhambra House, 27–31 Charing Cross Road, London WC2H OLS

Text © Ursula Ferrigno 2003 **Photography** © Peter Cassidy 2003 **Concept, edited text, design & layout** © Quadrille Publishing Ltd 2003

ISBN 0-8478-2547-7   Library of Congress Control Number 2002115808   Printed and bound by Dai Nippon in Hong Kong

3
all'istante
instant page 32

4
per tutti i giorni
everyday page 56

6
in anticipo
cook ahead page 106

7
impressionante
pasta to impress page 130

index page 158   acknowledgments page 160

le fondamenta basics

In Italy, hardly a meal is served without pasta and it has also become incredibly popular all over the world. It is, after all, inexpensive, quick to cook, highly nutritious, and extremely versatile. The range of dried and fresh pastas readily available from supermarkets and delicatessens today is seemingly endless, and, of course, you can combine these with all manner of really tasty sauces.

Pasta is an ancient food, and cave drawings in Imperia, northern Italy, suggest that it was there long before Marco Polo reportedly brought it back from China. Pasta is fundamental to Italian life. It is a daily ritual, consumed at every lunch or dinner, even on Christmas day, as part of the first course, *primo piatto*, after the *antipasti*, and before the main course, and never as a whole meal on its own.

Pasta was once a southern specialty, while in the north Italians favored rice and polenta, but pasta has somehow united Italy, and it is now eaten the length and breadth of the country. Pasta is the soul of Italian life. During the Renaissance, pasta—especially lasagne, ravioli, and tortellini—was found only on the tables of the wealthy. In the nineteenth century, however, it came to be viewed as food for the poor, especially in Naples. In the twentieth century, Mussolini went so far as to consider banning it from the Italian army's diet because he thought it made the soldiers lethargic!

From a nutritional angle, pasta is essentially a complex-carbohydrate food, but, because it has a low fat content, it isn't high in calories at all. (Of course, some of the sauces served with it can be.) Some varieties of pasta, notably those made with eggs, contain as much as 13 percent protein, as well as useful vitamins and minerals.

Let your imagination run riot with ingredients for a pasta sauce: Use vegetables, legumes, cheeses, oils, herbs, and spices. I eat pasta daily; it's the only thing I know I will definitely do each day. As my grandfather used to say, "I'm not living if I haven't eaten pasta every day."

Types of pasta

Fresh egg pasta (*pasta fresca all'uovo*) bought vacuum-sealed can be limp and tasteless, but Italian food stores that make pasta on the premises sell something closer to the real thing. Dried pasta (*pasta secca*) is good, especially if made in Italy from durum semolina (*pasta di semola di grano duro secca*), and there are types of dried egg pasta (*pasta all'uovo secca*). The ultimate pasta, however, is homemade. Most of the recipes I have included in this book use the simple pastas, such as spaghetti, tagliatelle, and lasagne—those that are most often used at home (*a casa*) in Italy. This keeps half-used packages of different shapes from cluttering up your cupboards.

Making pasta

Pasta should be made from hard flour rich in the gluten that gives pasta its true texture. In Italy, the wheat is very finely milled to produce 00-grade flour, which is fine and silky. It is available from good Italian delis. All-purpose flour can be used, but the pasta will be softer.

Basic egg pasta   makes about 2¼ pounds

This amount will make enough to serve 12 (it is easier to deal with larger quantities). Keep the dough in the refrigerator for several days, or freeze what you don't need immediately.

2½ cups flour, preferably Italian
00-grade (see above)
2½ cups semolina flour
1 teaspoon sea salt
7 large eggs (preferably corn-fed, so
the yolks are deep yellow)
2 tablespoons olive oil

1 Pile the flours on your countertop, then blend them together, adding the salt, and shape into a large volcanolike mound with a well in the middle.

2 Break the eggs into the well and add the oil. With a fork, slowly break up the eggs and draw in the flour to make a paste. When all the flour is mixed in you should have a ball of dough—if it seems too dry, add a little more oil or water; if it seems too damp, knead in a little more flour.

3 At first the mixture will be soft and claggy, but knead it until it is smooth and silken, and when you press a finger into it the depression bounces back. Wrap the dough in plastic wrap and let rest in the refrigerator about 30 minutes.

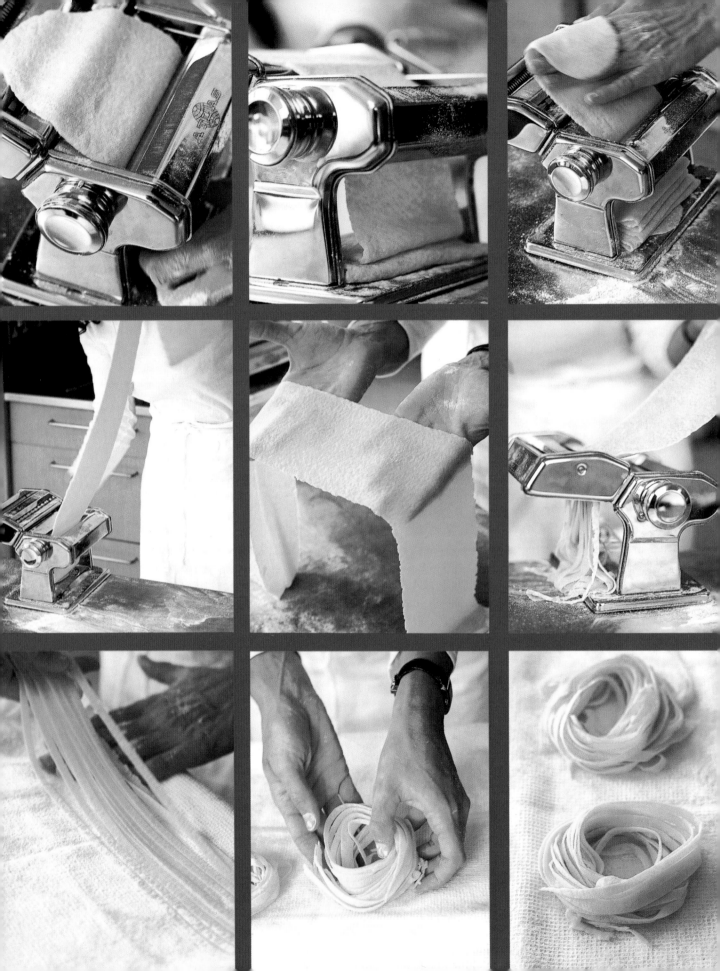

Using a pasta machine

Roll out the rested, chilled pasta dough to a long, thin oval that will just fit into the width of the pasta machine. Starting with the machine rollers set at their widest setting, pass the dough through the machine several times.

Change the machine rollers to the next thinnest setting and repeat the process. Continue down the settings in this way. By the time you have passed the dough several times through the setting one up from the thinnest (I never use the thinnest setting, because I find it produces pasta so fine it is too difficult to handle), the pasta should be ready for shaping. It should be thin enough for you to be able to make out the impression of your fingers through the sheet, as shown.

For shapes such as ravioli and lasagne, use these pasta sheets just as they are, trimming them to the required shape. To make noodles, however, pass the rolled-out dough through the selected cutters to produce the shape required. Leave to dry in lengths for 5 to 7 minutes (otherwise the pasta will stick to itself), then wind handfuls of the lengths of pasta into nests, as shown, and leave them to dry again briefly before cooking.

For pasta nero (squid ink pasta): simply add one ¼-ounce package squid ink with the eggs and oil. Packages of squid ink are sold at good fishmongers and in Italian delis.

For pasta verde or pasta con spinaci (spinach pasta): Replace 2 of the eggs with 18 ounces spinach cooked in a tightly closed pan (just in the water clinging to it after washing) for a few minutes until tender and then left to cool. You need to remove as much moisture from it as possible (squeeze it

Matching sauces to pasta shapes

Pasta is made in hundreds of different shapes, each one with a different ability to hold onto the all-important sauce. A simple rule of thumb is that hollow or twisted shapes take chunky sauces, and the flatter the pasta, the richer the sauce. Thin and long pasta suits an oily, more liquid sauce; more complicated shapes have holes and curves in which a thicker sauce can nestle and cling. In fact, new pastas designed to enhance the "cling" effect are introduced almost as regularly as the new, ever-more-clingy fashions modeled on Milan's catwalks.

Heavy sauces with large chunks of meat are unlikely to go well with thin spaghettini or tagliolini, simply because the chunks will slide off, so these sauces are always served with wide pasta such as pappardelle, maccheroni, and tagliatelle or with short, tubular shapes, such as penne, fusilli, conchiglie, and rigatoni.

In the south of Italy, olive oil is used for cooking rather than butter, so sauces there tend to be made with olive oil, and the sauces are usually served with dried plain durum wheat pasta (*pasta di semola grano duro*), such as spaghetti and vermicelli. These long, thin shapes are traditionally served with tomato and seafood sauces, most of which are made with olive oil, and with light vegetable sauces. Spaghetti and vermicelli are also ideal vehicles for minimalist sauces like *Aglio e Olio* from Rome (page 34). Grated cheese is not normally used in these sauces, nor is it sprinkled over them.

In the north, however, butter and cream are used in sauces and, not surprisingly, these go well with the egg pasta made in the region, which absorbs butter and cream to hold the sauce. Butter and cream also go well with tomato sauces when these are served with short shapes, especially penne, rigatoni, farfalle, and fusilli.

Cooking pasta

Cook the pasta in rapidly boiling water, bring the water back to a boil as quickly as possible, and keep at a rolling boil until the pasta is al dente. Always cook dried pasta in a large pot so there is plenty of room for the pasta to expand, as it absorbs water during cooking. Only salt the water when it is boiling; if the salt is put in too early it will disperse around the sides of the pan and the water will not be salty enough.

Dried pasta, which is made from durum wheat, is ready when it is al dente (literally "to the tooth")—that is, tender, but with a central resistance to the bite. You will see I have repeated this instruction in full in every recipe, and for this I make no apology. I watched my esteemed fellow Italian food writer Antonio Carluccio being criticized on a television program in which members of the public were asked to cook from one of his books. Even though he had carefully explained the phrase al dente in the introduction to the book, the readers still complained that since they did not know Italian, they didn't know quite what to do.

Fresh pasta, which is made from a softer wheat, is never as firm as dried when cooked, but it should still have some resistance. Overcooked pasta of any kind is limp and unpalatable, and an Italian cook would never serve it.

Stuffed pasta shapes require gentle handling or they can burst and release their filling into the water. Accordingly, add them to the boiling water, bring it back to a boil as quickly as possible, and then reduce the heat and poach the pasta shapes at a gentle simmer, stirring carefully during cooking.

When cooking spaghetti and other long dried pasta, you need to coil the pasta into the boiling water as it softens. Take a handful at a time and dip it in the boiling water so it touches the bottom of the pan. As the spaghetti strands soften, coil them around, using a wooden spoon or fork, until they are all completely submerged.

Amounts of pasta to cook
per person
DRIED PASTA 3 to 4 ounces
FRESH PASTA 4 to 5 ounces
FILLED PASTA 6 to 7 ounces

Cooking bought fresh pasta is generally much quicker, and can cook in as little as 4 to 5 minutes, although this will depend on the shape and size. Homemade tagliatelle, for example, can actually cook in as little as 30 seconds.

I actually cook my pasta in bottled Italian water whenever possible. It's terribly extravagant, but the pasta tastes amazing.

Serving pasta

The most important thing of all is to have your family and friends waiting at the table for the pasta, not the other way around. Pasta waits for no one. Cook it, dress it, and serve it at once. In Italy, pasta is served in a deep plate, which prevents the sauce from splashing and helps to keep the pasta warm, and the pasta is never served in a huge mound. Recipes vary in the way they combine sauce and pasta. The majority add the sauce to the pasta. The only hard-and-fast rule, however, is to always have warm bowls ready.

Freshly grated Parmesan cheese, the best being Parmigiano-Reggiano, is sprinkled on a great number of pasta dishes, enhancing the nutritional benefits with its added protein and calcium. It is not, however, traditionally added to most mushroom or fish and shellfish pasta dishes.

Eating pasta

Do it with a fork only, please, using it to lift the pasta and sauce together. Make a small space at the side of your plate and twist. The trick is to twizzle only a small amount around the fork at a time. *Buon appetito!*

2

zuppe e minestre

soups & stocks

Pasta in soup is very much a part of traditional Italian home cooking, although its role in this respect is greatly overlooked abroad. Served as a *primo piatto* instead of an ordinary pasta dish, it is seen as highly digestible, energy-giving food for fuel. Usually with lots of added vegetables and/or legumes, it makes the ultimate comfort food in winter. Importantly, Italians don't see soups as a repository for leftovers, but use the best and freshest of ingredients and put some energy into making the tastiest of stocks on which to base their pasta *in brodo*.

Minestrone alla Genovese Genoese Minestrone (with Pesto)   serves 4 to 6

In Genoa, cooks often make minestrone like this, with some of their local pesto stirred into the soup toward the end of cooking. Maltagliati, literally meaning "badly cut," are pasta from Emilia-Romagna made by cutting sheets of pasta into irregular shapes; small pieces are often used in soup.

1 onion

2 celery stalks

2 carrots

3 tablespoons olive oil

1 cup thin green beans cut into 2-inch pieces

1 zucchini, thinly sliced

1 potato, cut into 1/2-inch cubes

1/4 head savoy cabbage, shredded

1 cup cooked or rinsed canned cannellini beans

2 Italian plum tomatoes, chopped

1 1/4 quarts vegetable stock (page 19)

sea salt and freshly ground black pepper

3 1/2 ounces dried vermicelli or maltagliati (see above)

FOR THE PESTO

1 garlic clove

2 teaspoons pine nuts

2 tablespoons extra-virgin olive oil

1 tablespoon freshly grated Parmesan cheese

1 tablespoon freshly grated pecorino cheese

20 basil leaves

1 Chop the onion, celery, and carrots finely. Heat the oil in a large pot over low heat. Add the chopped vegetables and fry, stirring frequently, 5 to 7 minutes.

2 Stir in the green beans, zucchini, potato, and cabbage. Stir-fry over medium heat about 3 minutes. Add the cannellini beans and tomatoes and stir-fry 2 to 3 minutes longer.

3 Pour in the stock and add salt and pepper to taste. Bring to a boil, stir well, cover, and simmer, stirring occasionally, until all the vegetables are tender, about 40 minutes.

4 Meanwhile, make the pesto using a mortar and pestle: pound the garlic together with the pine nuts, then add the oil, cheeses, and basil, in that order, pounding until you have a thick sauce. You can use a food processor, but the flavor will not be as pungent.

5 Break the pasta into small pieces and add it to the soup. Simmer, stirring frequently, 5 minutes. Add the pesto and stir it in, then simmer 2 to 3 minutes longer or until the pasta is al dente, or tender but still firm to the bite.

6 Taste and adjust the seasoning, if necessary. Serve the minestrone in warm bowls.

Variation

You can dress the soup with any of the other versions of pesto in the book, such as Roasted Red Bell Pepper Pesto or Wild Arugula Pesto (see pages 111 – 12).

Minestrone di Pasta e Ceci Minestrone with Pasta and Chickpeas serves 4 to 6

Typical of the Molise region, this recipe delivers double carbohydrates for long-term energy. The flavor of rosemary works well with almost all types of legumes.

4 tablespoons olive oil

I onion, finely chopped

2 carrots, finely chopped

2 celery stalks, finely chopped

2½ cups cooked or rinsed canned chickpeas

I cup cooked or rinsed canned cannellini beans

⅔ cup tomato puree

2 fresh rosemary sprigs

7 ounces conchiglie

freshly grated Parmesan cheese, to serve

FOR THE VEGETABLE STOCK

I onion, halved

7 cloves

3 celery stalks

2 carrots

2 or 3 leeks

handful potato peelings, well cleaned

2 garlic cloves, halved

a little olive oil

3 fresh bay leaves, torn

handful fresh flat-leaf parsley with stems

sea salt and freshly ground black pepper

1 First make the vegetable stock: stud the onion halves with the cloves and coarsely chop the other vegetables and potato peelings. Heat the oil in a large heavy-bottom saucepan. Add all the vegetables and sauté until lightly colored. Add the remaining ingredients with cold water to cover and very lightly season with salt and pepper. Bring to a boil, skim well, lower the heat, and simmer gently, uncovered, 25 to 35 minutes.

2 Toward the end of the simmering time, heat the 4 tablespoons oil in a large saucepan over low heat. Add the finely chopped vegetables and sauté, stirring frequently, 5 to 7 minutes.

3 Add the chickpeas and cannellini beans, stir well to mix, then continue sautéing 5 minutes. Stir in the tomato puree and ½ cup water and simmer, stirring, 2 to 3 minutes.

4 Strain the stock, discarding the solids. Add 2½ cups of the stock, one of the rosemary sprigs, and salt and pepper to taste. Bring to a boil, then cover and simmer gently, stirring occasionally, I hour.

5 Add the remaining stock and the pasta. Bring to a boil, stirring, then lower the heat and simmer, stirring frequently, until the pasta is al dente, or tender but still firm to the bite, 7 to 8 minutes. Taste and adjust the seasoning.

6 Remove the rosemary sprig and serve the soup hot in warm bowls, topped with the cheese and fresh rosemary leaves.

Variation
Instead of the chickpeas, you can use a variety of other legumes, such as borlotti or even butter beans.

Minestra con Pasta e Verdure Arrostite Minestrone with Pasta and Roasted Vegetables

serves 4 to 6

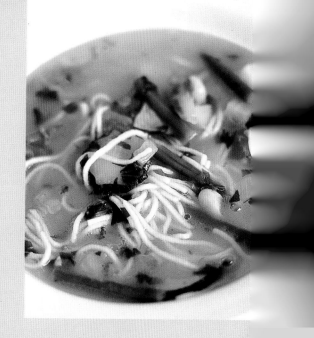

This is a classic Italian family dish with a twist. Every Italian home has its own version of the *minestra,* which means nothing more than "mixture." As there is no real fixed format, you can use whatever you like, whatever you have on hand and, preferably, whatever vegetables are in season.

7 tablespoons fresh ripe tomatoes (plum or vine-ripened)

3 tablespoons olive oil

1 onion

2 celery stalks

2 carrots

sea salt and freshly ground black pepper

1 potato, cut into ½-inch cubes

1 zucchini, thinly sliced

¼ head savoy cabbage, shredded

1 cup thin green beans, cut into 2-inch pieces

3 garlic cloves, finely chopped

3 fresh bay leaves

1 cup cooked or rinsed canned cannellini beans

1¼ quarts vegetable stock (page 19)

3½ ounces dried vermicelli or maltagliati (see page 18)

freshly grated Parmesan cheese, to serve

1 Heat the oven to 400°F.

2 Remove the stems and place the tomatoes in a roasting pan. Drizzle with a little of the oil and roast 20 to 30 minutes, depending on the tomato size, until they begin to color and the skins split. Remove from the oven and let cool slightly, then peel off the skins and chop the tomatoes roughly.

3 Dice the onion, celery, and carrots. Drizzle a little oil over and mix to coat the vegetables lightly. Season with salt and pepper, spread in a single layer on a baking tray, and roast 5 to 10 minutes. Add the potato and zucchini and return to the oven 5 to 10 minutes longer, until the onion and carrots are starting to caramelize and the zucchini and potatoes are lightly browned.

4 Heat the remaining oil in a large pot. Add the cabbage, green beans, and garlic and stir-fry 3 minutes. Add the bay leaves, cannellini beans, and all the roasted vegetables, then pour in the stock with salt and pepper to taste. Bring to a boil, stir well, cover, and simmer 30 minutes or so, stirring occasionally, until the vegetables are tender.

5 Break the pasta into small pieces and add to the soup. Simmer, stirring frequently, 6 to 8 minutes, or until the pasta is al dente, or just tender but still firm to the bite. Taste and adjust the seasoning, if necessary. Serve in warm bowls, sprinkled with cheese.

minestrone primavera (with spring vegetables)

Roast the onion, celery, and carrots to develop a good base flavor, then stir-fry I cup each podded fresh peas, chopped thin green beans, chopped plum tomatoes, and sliced zucchini with the garlic (omit the cabbage). Finish as for the basic recipe, with or without the beans.

minestrone di fagioli (with beans)

Make the soup base with the onion, celery, and carrots. Omit all the other vegetables, but add I cup each cooked or rinsed canned borlotti beans and chickpeas with the cannellini beans. Finish with lots of chopped fresh flat-leaf parsley.

minestrone inverno (with autumn/winter vegetables)

Make the soup base with the onion, celery, and carrots. Use ¹/₂ head savoy cabbage, shredded, and I cup each chopped turnip, winter squash, potatoes, and carrots instead of the green beans and zucchini. (You can roast the winter vegetables, if you like.) You can add cooked or rinsed canned cannellini or borlotti beans, if you like.

minestrone estate (with summer vegetables, and red and green bell peppers) Roast 3 bell peppers (2 red and 1 green) with the tomatoes. Peel off the charred skins, remove the seeds, and chop the peppers like the tomatoes; reserve any juices and add to the soup. Add other summer vegetables as you wish, making sure you include a zucchini (2 would be even better), and proceed as with the basic recipe.

Millescosedde Pasta, Bean, & Vegetable Soup   serves 4 to 6

The name of this Calabrian specialty comes from the Italian word *millescose*, meaning "a thousand things." Literally anything edible can go in this soup. In Calabria, cooks include a bean called *cicerchia*, which can be found only in that region; here I use cannellini beans and chickpeas.

$\frac{1}{2}$ cup brown lentils

3 fresh bay leaves

$\frac{1}{2}$ ounce dried mushrooms

4 tablespoons olive oil

1 carrot, diced

1 celery stalk, diced

1 onion, finely chopped

1 garlic clove, finely chopped

handful fresh flat-leaf parsley, chopped

pinch dried red chile flakes (optional)

$1\frac{1}{2}$ quarts vegetable stock (page 19)

1 cup cooked or rinsed canned cannellini beans

1 cup cooked or rinsed canned chickpeas

sea salt and freshly ground black pepper

1 cup dried small pasta shapes

freshly grated pecorino cheese, to serve

chopped fresh flat-leaf parsley, to garnish

1 Put the lentils in a medium-size saucepan over high heat with the bay leaves. Add 2 cups water and bring to a boil. Lower the heat to a gentle simmer and simmer, stirring occasionally, 15 to 20 minutes, or until the lentils are just tender.

2 Meanwhile, soak the dried mushrooms in $\frac{3}{4}$ cup warm water 15 to 20 minutes.

3 Drain the lentils, then rinse under cold water; set aside. Reserving the soaking liquid, drain the mushrooms. Finely chop the mushrooms and set aside.

4 Heat the oil in a large pot over low heat. Add the carrot, celery, onion, garlic, parsley, and chile flakes, if using. Stir-fry, stirring constantly, 5 to 7 minutes. Add the stock, then the mushrooms and their soaking liquid. Bring to a boil and add the beans, chickpeas, and lentils, with salt and pepper to taste. Cover and simmer gently 20 minutes.

5 Add the pasta, bring the soup back to a boil, stirring frequently, and cook 7 to 8 minutes, until the pasta is al dente, or tender but still firm to the bite.

6 Adjust the seasoning, then serve hot in soup bowls, with the cheese and parsley.

Variations
You can make this soup with any seasonal vegetables and a variety of other legumes, including borlotti and fava beans.

Zuppa di Lenticchie e Pastina Lentil and Pasta Soup serves 4 to 6

1 cup brown lentils

3 garlic cloves

3 tablespoons olive oil

2 tablespoons butter

1 onion, finely chopped

2 celery stalks, finely chopped

2 tablespoons sun-dried tomato paste

1¼ quarts vegetable stock (page 19)

a few fresh marjoram leaves

a few fresh basil leaves

leaves from 1 fresh thyme sprig

sea salt and freshly ground black pepper

⅓ cup dried small pasta shapes

herb leaves, to garnish

1 Put the lentils in a large pot. Smash 1 garlic clove and add it and 1 quart water to the lentils. Bring to a boil, lower the heat to a gentle simmer, and simmer, stirring occasionally, 20 minutes, or until the lentils are just tender. Drain the lentils and remove and discard the garlic. Rinse the lentils under cold water, then drain again.

2 Heat 2 tablespoons of the oil with half of the butter in a large pot over low heat. Add the onion and celery and sauté over low heat, stirring frequently, 5 to 7 minutes, until soft. Crush the remaining garlic, then peel it and add it to the vegetables with the remaining oil, the tomato paste, and the lentils. Stir, then add the stock, the fresh herbs, and salt and pepper to taste. Bring to a boil, stirring. Lower the heat and simmer 30 minutes, stirring occasionally.

3 Add the pasta and bring back to a boil, stirring. Lower the heat and simmer, stirring frequently, until the pasta is al dente, or tender but still firm to the bite, 7 to 8 minutes. Add the remaining butter, then taste and adjust the seasoning. Serve hot in warm bowls, sprinkled with herb leaves.

Zuppa Casalinga Farmhouse Soup serves 4 to 6

2 tablespoons olive oil

1 onion, roughly chopped

3 carrots

7 ounces turnips

6 ounces rutabagas

one 14½-ounce can crushed tomatoes

1 tablespoon tomato paste

handful mixed fresh herbs, such as rosemary, thyme, and flat-leaf parsley

1 teaspoon dried oregano

1½ quarts vegetable stock (page 19)

sea salt and freshly ground black pepper

⅓ cup dried small macaroni

2½ cups cooked or rinsed canned borlotti or cannellini beans

handful fresh flat-leaf parsley, to garnish

freshly grated Parmesan, to serve

1 Heat the oil in a large pot over low heat. Add the onion and fry, stirring frequently, about 5 minutes, until soft.

2 Cut all the fresh vegetables into large chunks, then add them to the pot along with the canned tomatoes, tomato paste, fresh herbs, and dried oregano. Pour in the stock, season with salt and pepper to taste, and bring to a boil. Stir well, cover, lower the heat, and simmer for 30 minutes, stirring occasionally.

3 Add the pasta and bring to a boil, stirring. Lower the heat and simmer, uncovered and stirring frequently, until the pasta is just al dente, or tender but still firm to the bite, about 5 minutes.

4 Stir in the beans and heat through, 2 to 3 minutes, then remove from the heat and stir in the parsley. Taste the soup and adjust the seasoning.

5 Serve hot in warm soup bowls, with the cheese handed around separately.

Pesce con Fregula Sardinian Fish Stew   serves 4 to 6

This Sardinian specialty is a cross between a soup and a stew. Fregula is actually a type of couscous, but small soup pasta can also be used. Serve with Italian country bread to mop up the delicious broth.

5 tablespoons olive oil

4 garlic cloves, finely chopped

½ small fresh red chile, seeded and finely chopped

1 large handful fresh flat-leaf parsley, roughly chopped

1 red snapper, about 1 pound, cleaned, head and tail removed

1 red or gray mullet, about 1¼ pounds, cleaned, head and tail removed

12 ounces to 1 pound thick cod fillet

one 14-ounce can chopped Italian plum tomatoes

sea salt and freshly ground black pepper

6 ounces dried fregula (see above), pastina, or pantaletti

1 Heat 2 tablespoons of the oil in a large Dutch oven over medium heat. Add the garlic, chile, and about half of the parsley. Sauté, stirring occasionally, about 5 minutes, taking care not to brown the garlic.

2 Cut all of the fish into large chunks, leaving the skin and bones in place in the case of the snapper and mullet, adding the pieces to the Dutch oven as you cut them. Sprinkle with 2 tablespoons of the oil, and sauté a few minutes longer.

3 Add the tomatoes, then fill the empty can with water and pour it into the Dutch oven. Bring to a boil. Stir in salt and pepper to taste, lower the heat, and cook 10 minutes, stirring occasionally.

4 Add the fregula or pasta and simmer 5 minutes. Add 1 cup water and the remaining oil and simmer 15 minutes longer.

5 If the soup becomes too thick, add more water. Taste and adjust the seasoning. Serve hot in warm bowls, sprinkled with the remaining parsley.

Zuppa di Vongole e Pastina Clam and Pasta Soup   serves 4 to 6

Subtly sweet and spicy, this soup is substantial enough to be served on its own for lunch or supper. A crusty loaf is my favorite accompaniment.

8 ounces raw clams
a little flour
2 tablespoons olive oil
I onion, finely chopped
leaves from I fresh thyme sprig, plus extra to garnish
2 garlic cloves, crushed
5 or 6 fresh basil leaves, torn, plus extra to garnish
½ teaspoon dried chile flakes
I quart fish stock
1½ cups tomato puree
I teaspoon sugar
sea salt and freshly ground black pepper
½ cup shelled fresh peas
½ cup dried small pasta shapes

1 Keep the clams submerged in water with a little added flour (to help plump them up and purge them of any dirt). Discard any that remain open when tapped.

2 Heat the oil in a large pot over medium heat. Add the onion and cook slowly, stirring, about 5 minutes, until soft but not colored. Add the thyme, then stir in the garlic, basil, chile flakes, stock, tomato puree, sugar, and salt and pepper to taste. Bring to a boil, then lower the heat and simmer, stirring occasionally, 15 minutes. Add the peas and simmer 5 minutes longer.

3 Add the pasta and bring to a boil, stirring. Lower the heat and simmer, stirring frequently, until the pasta is only just al dente, or tender but still firm to the bite, about 5 minutes.

4 Discard any open clams that do not close when tapped. Turn the heat down to low, add the clams, and continue simmering 5 to 7 minutes, until the clams open. Taste and adjust the seasoning.

5 Serve the soup hot, garnished with extra basil and thyme.

Variation
If pressed, you can make a fairly reputable version of this dish with canned clams — but look for an Italian brand and rinse them well! Flavorful clams in brine are also widely available in supermarkets.

Pastina in Brodo Pasta in Meat Broth   serves 4

about I pound meat bones (any type, or a mixture, will do — ask your butcher)

3 fresh bay leaves

sea salt and freshly ground black pepper

2 ripe tomatoes

2¼ ounce small soup pasta, such as farfalline (little farfalle, see page 45)

I tablespoon extra-virgin olive oil

2 tablespoons freshly grated Parmesan cheese

handful fresh flat-leaf parsley, finely chopped

1 Heat the oven to 400°F. Put the bones in a large roasting pan and roast 25 minutes, or until well colored.

2 Put the browned bones in a large pot and cover with water. Add the bay leaves and season with salt. Bring to a boil, skim well, and then simmer slowly, uncovered, 40 minutes, skimming from time to time if necessary. Strain.

3 Meanwhile, put the tomatoes in a bowl and cover with boiling water about 40 seconds, then drain and plunge them into cold water. Using a sharp knife, peel off the skins and finely chop the flesh, discarding the seeds.

4 Add the tomatoes to the stock and simmer 2 to 3 minutes longer.

5 Bring to a boil and stir in the pasta. Simmer 3 to 5 minutes, until the pasta is just tender. Season with salt and pepper to taste and stir in the oil.

6 Serve hot, sprinkled with the cheese and parsley.

Pasta in Brodo con Piselli e Fegatini Pasta Soup with Peas and Chicken Livers   serves 4 to 6

4 ounces fresh chicken livers

3 sprigs fresh flat-leaf parsley

3 sprigs fresh marjoram

3 sprigs fresh sage

leaves from I sprig fresh thyme

I tablespoon olive oil

knob unsalted butter

4 garlic cloves, crushed

sea salt and freshly ground black pepper

I to 2 tablespoons dry white wine

I¼ quarts chicken stock

4 medium-size potatoes, peeled and cubed

I⅓ cups shelled fresh peas

⅓ cup dried pasta shapes, such as farfalle (see page 45)

handful fresh basil leaves

1 Trim the chicken livers and cut them into small pieces (this is best done with scissors). Chop the herbs.

2 Heat the oil and butter in a skillet over medium heat. Add the garlic and herbs, with salt and pepper to taste, and sauté, stirring, a few minutes. Add the livers, increase the heat to high, and sauté a few minutes, until they change color and become dry. Pour the wine over and cook until it evaporates. Remove the pan from the heat, taste, and adjust the seasoning.

3 Put the chicken stock in a large pot with some salt and pepper and bring to a boil. Add the potatoes and the peas and simmer 5 minutes, then add the pasta. Bring the soup back to a boil, stirring. Lower the heat and simmer, stirring frequently, until the pasta is just al dente, or tender but still firm to the bite, about 5 minutes.

4 Add the liver mixture and the basil and warm through. Adjust the seasoning and serve hot in warm bowls.

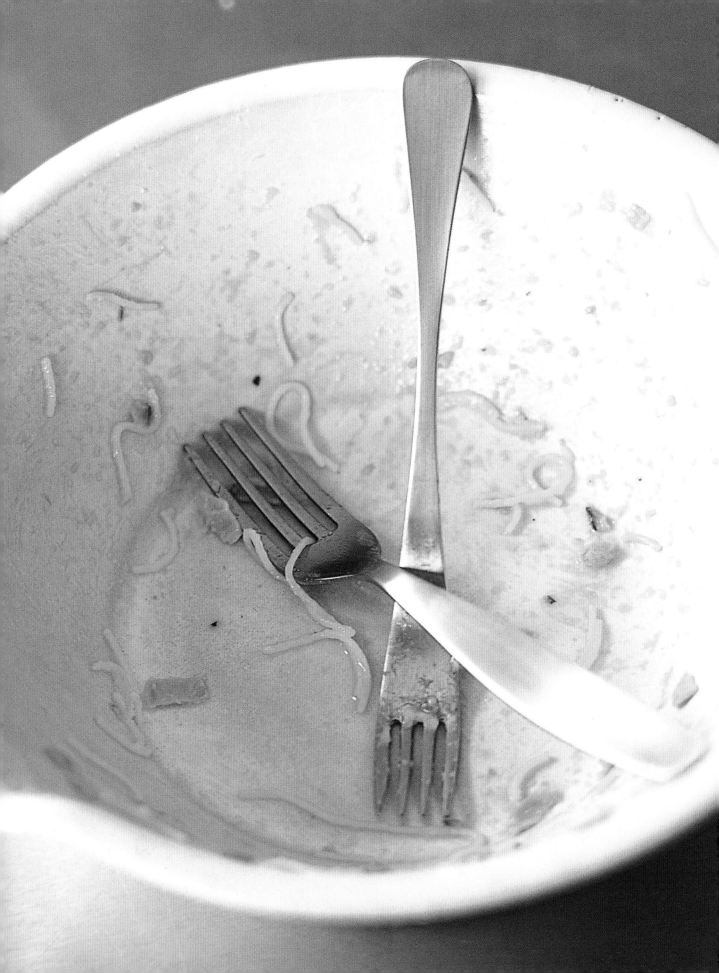

3 all'istante

instant

Pasta is one of the easiest of foods to cook in a hurry. In the 10 minutes or so it takes to cook most dried pastas, lots of wonderful, tasty sauces can be made. Some can even be put together in the few minutes that fresh pasta needs, and some can literally be made at the table. The secret to enjoying any number of fast pasta dishes is having the correct ingredients in your cupboard, like good oil, canned Italian plum tomatoes, canned cannellini or borlotti beans or chickpeas, and cans of anchovies, tuna, and clams. With a good chunk of Parmesan in the refrigerator, together with eggs, cream, and possibly some bacon or pancetta, and you can conjure up a veritable feast. A couple of fresh herbs, such as parsley, chives, and basil, will help heighten the magic.

Spaghetti con Cacio e Pepe Spaghetti with Cheese and Pepper   serves 2

This Roman dish is the perfect cupboard stand-by.

7 ounces spaghetti
sea salt
little knob unsalted butter
4 tablespoons freshly grated Parmesan cheese
$\frac{1}{2}$ teaspoon freshly ground black pepper

1 Cook the pasta in a large pot of boiling salted water about 10 minutes, until al dente, or just tender but still firm to the bite.

2 Drain the pasta and transfer it to a warm serving bowl and add the butter, cheese, and pepper; stir well and serve straight away. It couldn't be simpler!

Pasta all'Aglio e Olio Pasta with Garlic and Oil   serves 2

Versions of this simple classic pop up all over Italy, and they are almost always more than acceptable. It is one of those dishes that most Italian families enjoy at least once a week, often as supper on Monday evenings.

7 ounces spaghetti
sea salt
2 garlic cloves, crushed
$\frac{1}{2}$ small fresh red chile, seeded and finely chopped, or 1 small dried chile pepper (peperoncino), crushed
4 to 5 tablespoons fruity or lemony extra-virgin olive oil
handful fresh flat-leaf parsley, finely chopped

1 Cook the pasta in a large pot of boiling salted water about 10 minutes, until al dente, or just tender but still firm to the bite.

2 Meanwhile, in a small bowl stir the garlic, chile, and a pinch of salt into the oil.

3 When the pasta is cooked, drain and quickly dress with the oil mixture. Serve immediately, sprinkled generously with the parsley.

Variation
You can make endless variations to this, adding more pungent flavorings, such as finely grated lemon zest, chopped capers, pitted olives, or rinsed anchovies.

Consiglio **To mask the smell of garlic on the breath, try a glass of milk, a handful of parsley, an apple, a strong espresso coffee, or a measure of Campari.**

Spaghetti con Pomodori Freschi Spaghetti with Fresh Tomato Sauce serves 2

To guarantee maximum flavor, use the reddest, ripest tomatoes you can find.

7 ounces spaghetti
sea salt and freshly ground black pepper
6 ripe tomatoes
2 garlic cloves, crushed
3 tablespoons olive oil
4 tablespoons freshly grated Parmesan cheese, plus extra to serve
handful torn fresh basil leaves

1 Cook the pasta in a large pot of boiling salted water about 10 minutes, until just al dente, or tender but still firm to the bite.

2 Meanwhile, chop the tomatoes and put them in a bowl with the garlic, oil, cheese, basil, and salt and pepper. Mix together.

3 Drain the pasta and toss it with the sauce. Serve immediately with extra grated cheese, if you wish.

Pasta alla Crudaiola Pasta with Raw Tomato Sauce serves 4

This is a wonderfully simple uncooked tomato sauce (*crudaiola* means "raw") that goes well with many different kinds of pasta, both longs strands and short shapes. However, I prefer it with long pasta, especially bucatini or spaghetti. It is always made in summer, when the plum tomatoes have ripened on the vine in the sun and have their fullest flavor.

12 ounces pasta of your choice
1¼ pounds ripe Italian plum tomatoes
1 large handful fresh basil leaves
5 tablespoons extra-virgin olive oil
¾ cup diced ricotta salata (firm ricotta; see Consiglio, below)
1 garlic clove, crushed
sea salt and freshly ground black pepper
coarsely shaved pecorino cheese, to serve

1 Cook the pasta in a large pot of boiling salted water about 10 minutes, until al dente, or just tender but still firm to the bite.

2 Meanwhile, roughly chop the tomatoes, removing the cores and as many of the seeds as you can. Tear the basil leaves into shreds with your fingers.

3 Put the tomatoes, basil, oil, ricotta, and garlic in a bowl, season with salt and pepper to taste, and stir well. (If you are not in a hurry, it is a good idea at this point to cover the bowl and leave at room temperature 1 to 2 hours, to let the flavors mingle. Obviously you wouldn't cook the pasta until then either.)

4 Taste the sauce and adjust the seasoning if necessary. Drain the pasta and toss it with the sauce. Serve immediately, with the pecorino handed around separately.

Consiglio **Ricotta salata is a salted and dried version of ricotta. Firmer than traditional soft white ricotta, it can easily be diced, crumbled, or grated. Young soft pecorino can be used in its place.**

Spaghetti al Mortaio Spaghetti with Pureed Tomatoes, Bell Pepper, Basil, and Mint   serves 4

'*Al mortaio*' actually means "in a mortar," and refers to the fact that this sauce is a puree. I make it in a blender, but originally it would have been pounded in a mortar with a pestle. This is one of those dishes in which the sauce's flavor is very much a function of the quality of the olive oil used.

13 ounces spaghetti

sea salt and freshly ground black pepper

1 pound, 5 ounces ripe tomatoes

½ garlic clove

1 sweet red bell pepper, seeded and sliced

handful fresh mint leaves

3 tablespoons fruity extra-virgin olive oil, ideally finest estate-bottled

handful fresh basil leaves

4 tablespoons freshly grated Parmesan cheese

1 Cook the pasta in a large pot of boiling salted water about 10 minutes, until just al dente, or tender but still firm to the bite.

2 Meanwhile, scald the tomatoes with boiling water, then peel them. Cut them in half and remove the seeds.

3 Place the tomatoes in a food processor with salt and pepper to taste, the garlic, bell pepper, and mint. Blend well, until the sauce becomes smooth and uniform. Adjust the seasoning, if necessary.

4 Drain the pasta well and return it to the pan. Add the oil, the pureed sauce, and the basil and mix well. Serve with the cheese.

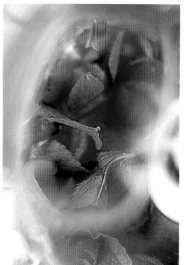

Penne con Fave e Ricotta Penne with Fava Beans and Ricotta   serves 4

This is a southern Italian treat in the springtime, when young, fresh fava beans are abundant. Don't try it with cooked dried fava beans. Very young beans are even eaten raw with pecorino. Most common in Liguria and Campania, penne are tube-shaped pasta cut at an angle to make them look like quills. Penne rigate, with ribbing on the outside of the quills, are among the best sauce retainers.

I cup shelled fresh fava beans

7 ounces penne

sea salt and freshly ground black pepper

I tablespoon olive oil

I garlic clove, crushed

2 tablespoons freshly grated pecorino cheese

¼ cup ricotta cheese

about 2 tablespoons extra-virgin olive oil

fresh marjoram leaves, to garnish

1 Steam the fava beans 6 minutes, or until tender.

2 Meanwhile, cook the pasta in a large pot of boiling salted water about 10 minutes, until just al dente, or tender but still firm to the bite.

3 Heat the 1 tablespoon olive oil in a large saucepan over medium heat. Add the garlic and sauté until light brown.

4 Drain the pasta and add it to the pan along with the fava beans, cheeses, extra-virgin olive oil, and salt and pepper to taste. Toss well.

5 Serve garnished with marjoram leaves.

Fettuccine all'Alfredo Alfredo's Fettuccine (with cream and cheese) serves 4

This simple recipe was invented in the 1920s by a Roman restaurateur named Alfredo, who became famous for serving it with a golden fork and spoon. You can use tagliatelle, which is what the northern Italians call fettuccine, although tagliatelle strips are slightly narrower.

4 tablespoons unsalted butter

1 cup heavy cream

4 tablespoons freshly grated Parmesan cheese, plus extra to serve

sea salt and freshly ground black pepper

12 ounces fresh fettuccine or tagliatelle

1 Melt the butter in a large saucepan over medium heat. Add the cream and bring to just below a boil. Simmer 5 minutes, stirring, then add the cheese, and salt and pepper to taste. Turn off the heat under the pan.

2 Meanwhile, bring a large pot of salted water to a boil. Drop in the pasta all at once and quickly bring back to a boil, stirring occasionally. Boil 2 to 3 minutes, until al dente, or tender but firm to the bite; drain well.

3 Turn the heat under the pan of sauce to low. Add the pasta all at once and toss until it is coated in the sauce. Taste and adjust the seasoning. Serve at once with extra cheese.

Bucatini con Zucchini Bucatini with Zucchini serves 4

Long and thin, pale in color, and heavily ridged, Romanesco zucchini give the best results, so look out for imported ones in upscale gourmet food stores. Bucatini are the long hollow noodles, like slightly fatter spaghetti but with a hole down the middle to help them cook faster.

13 ounces bucatini

sea salt and freshly ground black pepper

2/3 cup extra-virgin olive oil

1 pound small, tender zucchini

1 cup freshly grated Parmesan cheese, plus more to serve, if you like

1 cup freshly grated sweet provolone cheese, plus more to serve, if you like

4 tablespoons unsalted butter, cut into little pieces

handful fresh basil leaves, torn

handful fresh mint leaves, torn

1 garlic clove, crushed

2 tablespoons fruity extra-virgin olive oil

1 Cook the bucatini in a large pot of boiling salted water about 10 minutes, until just al dente, or tender but still firm to the bite.

2 Meanwhile, heat the olive oil in a sauté pan. Cut the zucchini into thin slices and fry them, a few at a time, until light golden; transfer to a large bowl.

3 Add the cheeses, butter, basil, mint, and garlic to the bowl and season with salt and pepper to taste.

4 Drain the pasta thoroughly and toss well with the zucchini mixture.

5 Serve immediately, drizzled with the fruity extra-virgin olive oil and with extra cheese, if desired.

Rigatoni con Pignoli e Gorgonzola Rigatoni with Pine Nuts and Gorgonzola   serves 2

This northern dish makes the most of tasty gorgonzola. I prefer it made with sharp gorgonzola piccante, but you can try the *dolce* variety if you prefer a milder cheese flavor. Rigatoni are large pasta tubes which are ribbed on the exterior. Their size and shape suit strongly flavored sauces.

½ cup broccoli florets
½ cup cauliflower florets
7 ounces rigatoni
sea salt and freshly ground black pepper
⅓ cup pine nuts
2 tablespoons olive oil
I red onion, finely chopped
I teaspoon chopped fresh thyme
4 ounces gorgonzola cheese

1 Steam the broccoli and cauliflower florets about 12 minutes, until tender.

2 At the same time, cook the rigatoni in a large pot of boiling salted water about 10 minutes, until just al dente or tender, but still firm to the bite.

3 Meanwhile, toast the pine nuts on a sheet of foil under a hot broiler, turning them frequently.

4 Heat the oil in a saucepan over medium heat. Add the onion and sauté until soft. Add the thyme, and salt and pepper to taste.

5 Cut the cheese into cubes and add it to the onion mixture, along with the pine nuts, broccoli, and cauliflower.

6 Drain the pasta and toss it with the vegetable mixture. Adjust the seasoning to taste and serve.

Variation
You can toast the pine nuts in a dry skillet over low heat. Keep your eye on them, though, because they can burn in the blink of an eye.

Consiglio Fusilli, spiral-shaped pasta, are equally good in this recipe, and 9 ounces cooked spinach can be used instead of the broccoli and cauliflower.

Conchiglie con Salsa di Noci e Funghi Pasta Shells with Walnut and Mushroom Sauce   serves 4

This wonderfully light and luscious recipe from the Parma region of Italy combines two of my all-time favorite flavors. Conchiglie are the familiar pasta shells which, because of their receptacle-like shape and the fact that they are ribbed, really mop up a sauce.

4 ounces dried wild mushrooms, preferably porcini
12 ounces conchiglie
sea salt and freshly ground black pepper
½ cup walnuts
handful fresh basil leaves
handful fresh young sage leaves
1 cup light cream
1 large garlic clove
2 tablespoons unsalted butter
4 tablespoons freshly grated Parmesan cheese

1 Soak the dried mushrooms in warm water to cover 10 minutes.

2 Meanwhile, cook the pasta in a large pot of boiling salted water about 10 minutes, until al dente, or tender but still firm to the bite.

3 While the pasta cooks, finely chop the walnuts, tear the basil, and chop the sage. Add the cream and season with salt and pepper to taste; mix together.

4 Crush the garlic. Drain the mushrooms and pat dry, then chop any that are large. Melt the butter in a large skillet over medium-low heat. Add the garlic and sauté slowly 2 to 3 minutes. Stir in the mushrooms and walnut sauce and warm through without boiling.

5 Drain the pasta and pour the sauce over it, stirring well. Serve sprinkled with cheese.

Variations

If you are lucky enough to get fresh walnuts, still in the shell, make a simple pasta with walnut sauce using this recipe, but without the mushrooms. Replace the assertive basil and sage with a handful of chopped parsley to better set off the subtle flavor of the nuts. Store walnuts in the refrigerator or freezer to prevent them from becoming rancid.

For a version of either dish with fewer fat and calories, replace the cream with bread soaked in milk, and whiz it and the nuts in a food processor until the nuts are finely chopped.

Farfalle alla Crema di Gorgonzola Farfalle with Gorgonzola Cream serves 4

In Italy, bow-tie-shaped farfalle is the second favorite pasta shape after spaghetti, as it captures so much sauce and cooks quickly. It is perfect for a quick dish in which you simply stir in the sauce ingredients.

12 ounces dried farfalle
sea salt and freshly ground black pepper
1 cup very finely diced rinded gorgonzola cheese, at room temperature
¾ cup heavy cream
pinch sugar
2 teaspoons finely chopped fresh sage leaves, plus fresh sage leaves, shredded, to garnish

1 Cook the pasta in a large pot of boiling salted water 8 to 10 minutes, until just al dente, or tender but still firm to the bite.

2 Drain the pasta well and return it to the pot. Add the cheese, cream, sugar, plenty of black pepper, and the chopped sage. Toss, over medium heat, until the pasta is evenly coated. Taste and season with more salt, if necessary.

3 Divide among 4 warm bowls. Garnish each portion with sage and serve immediately.

Four cheeses **Instead of just the gorgonzola, simply stir in 2 ounces each Parmesan, Gruyère, fontina, and gorgonzola (grate the first two and dice the others very small) with the other additions.**

Cooked shrimp **Shell 12 ounces large cooked shrimp (7 ounces if already peeled) and stir these into the pasta with 2 crushed garlic cloves, the grated zest of 1 unwaxed lemon, and some fresh flat-leaf parsley instead of the sage.**

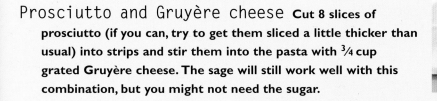

Prosciutto and Gruyère cheese **Cut 8 slices of prosciutto (if you can, try to get them sliced a little thicker than usual) into strips and stir them into the pasta with ¾ cup grated Gruyère cheese. The sage will still work well with this combination, but you might not need the sugar.**

Spinach and tomatoes **Rinse 1¼ pounds baby spinach leaves well and spin or pat dry. Seed and chop 8 ripe tomatoes, preferably Italian. Sir these into the pasta, together with 2 crushed garlic cloves and some fresh flat-leaf parsley instead of the sage.**

Fettuccine con Ceci Fettuccine with Chickpeas   serves 4

This is a classic Neapolitan dish. Chickpeas are grown all over Italy, but thrive in the south, where it is sunny. Although I think dried legumes have more flavor and texture, canned are definitely quick and easy and make a good substitute. If you have the time and can cook chickpeas (see the Variation, below), the flavor of this dish will be at its very best. However, bear in mind that the older the legume, the longer it will take to cook, and the flavor will not be as appetizing.

12 ounces fettuccine
sea salt and freshly ground black pepper
12 tasty, flavorful tomatoes, or
7 ounces vine-ripened cherry tomatoes
4 tablespoons olive oil
2 garlic cloves, crushed
generous handful fresh flat-leaf parsley, chopped
one 14-ounce can chickpeas, drained and rinsed
2 tablespoons fruity, fine extra-virgin olive oil
generous quantity freshly grated Parmesan cheese, to serve
generous handful fresh basil leaves, torn, to serve

1 Cook the pasta in a large pot of boiling salted water about 10 minutes, until just al dente, or tender, but still firm to the bite.

2 Meanwhile, put the tomatoes in a bowl and cover with boiling water about 40 seconds, then drain and plunge them into cold water. Using a sharp knife, peel off the skins and chop the flesh. If using vine-ripened cherry tomatoes, just halve.

3 Heat the olive oil in a medium-size saucepan over medium heat. Add the garlic and sauté until light golden. Add the tomatoes, parsley, chickpeas, and salt and pepper to taste; cover and set aside.

4 Drain the pasta and toss it in the fruity extra-virgin olive oil and the chickpea mixture. Adjust the seasoning to taste.

5 Serve in warm bowls with lots of cheese and basil leaves.

Variation
If you have the time to use dried chickpeas, soak $2/3$ cup dried chickpeas overnight in a bowl of cold water. The next day, drain and put them in a large pot. Cover with fresh water, bring to a boil, and boil 10 minutes. Lower the heat and simmer 20 to 30 minutes, until tender. Drain well and use like the canned.

Spaghetti alla Rancetto Spaghetti with Tomatoes and Pancetta   serves 4

This traditional dish gets its name from a restaurant in Spoleto, in Umbria. It uses a fresh and light sauce in which the tomatoes are cooked for a short time only. Always search out good, flavorful tomatoes, preferably from where the sun has been shining on them, because this will make a world of difference.

12 ounces ripe plum tomatoes
1 cup diced pancetta
2 tablespoons olive oil
1 onion, finely chopped
sea salt and freshly ground black pepper
12 ounces fresh or dried spaghetti
handful fresh marjoram sprigs, leaves stripped
generous amount freshly grated pecorino cheese, to serve

1 Chop the tomatoes into chunky dice.

2 Put the pancetta in a medium-size saucepan with the oil over low heat. Stir until the fat runs, then add the onion, stir to mix, and sauté about 5 minutes, stirring.

3 Add the tomatoes, and salt and pepper to taste. Stir well and simmer 7 minutes.

4 Meanwhile, cook the pasta a large pot of boiling salted water, until just al dente, or tender but still firm to the bite.

5 Remove the sauce from the heat and stir in the marjoram leaves. Taste and adjust the seasoning, if necessary.

6 Drain the pasta and transfer it to a warm serving bowl. Pour the sauce over the pasta and toss well. Serve immediately in warm bowls. Hand around the cheese separately.

Variation
Very similar is Amatriciana, a classic tomato sauce named after the town of Amatrice in the Sabine Hills, in Lazio. If you visit Rome, you will see it on many restaurant menus, served with either bucatini or spaghetti. Add a seeded and thinly sliced fresh red chile and replace the marjoram with 2 to 3 tablespoons dry white wine for a good approximation of the traditional sauce.

Consiglio   Try to find pancetta; bacon can be substituted, but the sauce will not taste the same. You can buy packages of diced pancetta in supermarkets and gourmet delicatessens. Alternatively, buy it in a single piece, sometimes cut from a roll (*arrotolata*), and dice it yourself.

Vermicelli allo Zafferano Vermicelli with Saffron   serves 4

This quick and easy dish makes a delicious midweek supper. The ingredients are likely to be sitting in your refrigerator, so it is also perfect for impromptu meals. Saffron strands are better than powder, because they have much more flavor.

12 ounces dried vermicelli
sea salt and freshly ground black
pepper
large pinch saffron strands
1 cup cooked ham cut
into strips
1 cup heavy cream
4 tablespoons freshly grated Parmesan
cheese, plus extra to serve
2 egg yolks

1 Cook the pasta in a large pot of boiling salted water about 10 minutes, until just al dente, or tender but still firm to the bite.

2 While the pasta is cooking, put the saffron strands in a saucepan over high heat. Add 2 tablespoons water and bring to a boil immediately. Remove the pan from the heat and set it aside for a while.

3 Add the ham to the pan containing the saffron, and stir in the cream and cheese with a little salt and pepper to taste. Heat slowly, stirring constantly. When the cream starts to bubble, remove the pan from the heat and add the egg yolks, beating well to mix. Taste and adjust the seasoning.

4 Drain the pasta and add it to the sauce; mix well. Serve in warm bowls, with extra cheese.

Variation
This dish is a really just a slightly upscale version of the classic Spaghetti alla Carbonara, named after the Roman charcoal workers who are said to have devised it. Without the glamorous touch of saffron and using ham or bacon, eggs, and cheese the same way, this sauce became one of the earliest pasta dishes to be well known outside Italy, as it was a firm favorite among Allied soldiers in Italy in the Second World War. It reminded the soldiers of their own homey breakfasts, so they took the recipe home with them.

Spaghetti alla Carrettiera Spaghetti with Mushrooms, Pancetta, and Tuna   serves 4

The term *carrettiera* means "in the style of a cart driver," as this is the sort of robust meal they would have ordered at a trattoria at the end of a long journey. The Romans lay claim to the recipe, but so do the Neapolitans and Sicilians, hence there are many different versions of it.

1 ounce dried porcini mushrooms
2 tablespoons olive oil
1 garlic clove
½ cup pancetta or streaky slab bacon cut into ¼-inch slices
3 cups chopped white mushrooms
sea salt and freshly ground black pepper
12 ounces dried spaghetti
one 7-ounce can tuna (preferably in olive oil), drained

1 Put the porcini in a small bowl with ¾ cup warm water and let soak 15 minutes.

2 Meanwhile, heat the oil in a large saucepan over medium heat. Add the garlic clove and fry slowly about 2 minutes, crushing it with a wooden spoon to release the flavor; remove and discard the garlic. Add the pancetta to the oil remaining in the pan and sauté 3 to 4 minutes, stirring occasionally.

3 Reserving the soaking liquid, drain the porcini and chop them finely.

4 Add the porcini and the white mushrooms to the pan and sauté 1 to 2 minutes. Add 6 tablespoons of the reserved mushroom soaking liquid, season to taste with salt and pepper and simmer 5 minutes.

5 Meanwhile, cook the pasta in boiling salted water combined with the remaining mushroom soaking liquid about 10 minutes, until al dente, or just tender but still firm to the bite.

6 Flake the tuna into the mushroom sauce and fold it in gently. Taste and adjust the seasoning, if necessary.

7 Drain the pasta well and transfer it to a warm serving bowl. Pour the sauce over the top and toss well. Serve immediately.

Variation
You can replace the canned tuna with canned sardines — or even some broiled or grilled fresh ones, if you feel like it,

Maccheroni alla Bottarga di Favignana Macaroni with Dried Tuna Roe serves 4

Although this may seem an unusual recipe, with bottarga—salted and air-dried mullet or tuna roe—as the principal ingredient, it is very well known in Sardinia, Sicily, and parts of southern Italy. It is simplicity itself to make and tastes very, very good. The raw garlic and pine nut *crema* with which the dish is dressed cuts the saltiness of the roe beautifully and can itself make a delicious dressing for plain pasta.

12 ounces maccheroni
sea salt and freshly ground black
pepper
2 tablespoons olive oil
1 garlic clove, sliced
10 cherry tomatoes, halved
½ glass dry white wine
handful flat-leaf parsley, chopped
2 tablespoons extra-virgin olive oil
**3 ounces bottarga di tonno, very
finely diced (see Consiglio, right)**

FOR THE CREMA
2 garlic cloves
2 tablespoons pine nuts,
preferably Italian

1 Cook the pasta in a large pot of boiling salted water about 10 minutes, until just al dente, or tender but still firm to the bite.

2 Meanwhile, make the crema: using a mortar and pestle, crush the garlic cloves and the pine nuts to a paste.

3 Heat the olive oil in a medium-size saucepan over medium heat. Add the sliced garlic, the tomatoes, and the wine and sauté 3 minutes, until the wine is absorbed.

4 Drain the pasta and toss it with the parsley, extra-virgin olive oil, and the bottarga. Add the tomato sauce and toss again.

5 Top with the crema and serve immediately.

Variation
Although this dish suits the firm stubbiness of maccheroni incredibly well, you can also make a version with spaghetti and dress it with a garlic-infused oil instead of the crema.

Consiglio Buy bottarga in Italian delicatessens. Small jars of grated bottarga are convenient, but the best flavor comes from vacuum-packed slices of mullet bottarga, which are very easy to grate. Keep any leftover bottarga lightly wrapped in the refrigerator.

per tutti i giorni
everyday

4

As I have said several times elsewhere in the book, like most Italians I don't regard it as a proper day unless I've had at least one plate of pasta. Everyday pasta is family fare, using the least expensive ingredients, such as seasonal vegetables and legumes. Flavoring ingredients like chiles and dried porcini also feature quite often, as they go a long way and deliver a lot of punch for pennies. Do not stint on buying the best and most flavorful oil, butter, and cheese—as well, obviously, as good, tasty (made-in-Italy) pasta!

Pasta con Piselli Pasta and Peas   serves 2

This simple *nonna* (grandmother)-style dish shows that the combination of peas and basil is as delightful as that of tomato and basil. Pappardelle are the wide pasta ribbons of the Veneto and Tuscany.

2 tablespoons olive oil

I small onion, finely chopped

I cup shelled fresh peas

2 cups vegetable stock, preferably homemade (page 19)

5 ounces pappardelle

sea salt and freshly ground black pepper

handful torn fresh basil leaves, to serve

Parmesan cheese, to serve

1 Heat the oil in a medium-size saucepan over medium heat. Add the onion and fry until soft. Add the peas and stock and simmer 10 minutes, until the peas are soft.

2 Add the pasta, broken into pieces, with some salt and pepper to taste. Bring to a boil, then lower the heat and cook about 12 minutes, until the pasta is al dente, or tender but still firm to the bite; it will absorb some of the stock.

3 Serve sprinkled with basil and lots of cheese.

Consiglio   To eat this at its best, use fresh new season's peas when they are sweet and tender.

Pasta con Sugo di Verdure Pasta with Green Vegetable Sauce   serves 4

Although described as *sugo* in Italian, this is not a true sauce, because it does not have any liquid apart from the oil and melted butter. It is more a medley of vegetables to toss with freshly cooked pasta.

2 carrots

I zucchini

3 ounces thin green beans

I small leek

2 ripe Italian plum tomatoes

handful fresh flat-leaf parsley

12 ounces pasta of your choice

sea salt and freshly ground black pepper

2 tablespoons butter

3 tablespoons extra-virgin olive oil

½ teaspoons sugar

⅔ cup shelled fresh peas

1 Finely dice the carrots and the zucchini. Top and tail the green beans, then cut them into ³/4-inch pieces. Thinly slice the leek. Scald the tomatoes with boiling water, drain, plunge them into cold water, then peel, seed, and dice them. Chop the parsley.

2 Cook the pasta in a large pot of boiling salted water about 10 minutes, until al dente, or just tender but still firm to the bite.

3 Melt the butter with the oil in a medium-size saucepan over medium heat. When the mixture sizzles, add the prepared leek and carrots. Sprinkle the sugar over and fry, stirring frequently, about 5 minutes. Stir in the zucchini, green beans, peas, and plenty of salt and pepper. Cover and cook over low to medium heat, stirring occasionally, 5 to 8 minutes, until the vegetables are tender.

4 Stir in the parsley and tomatoes and adjust the seasoning to taste. Drain the pasta, toss it with the vegetable mixture, and serve at once.

Spaghetti alla Bellini Spaghetti with Mushrooms   serves 4

This tasty dish is named after Pina Bellini, the celebrated proprietor of La Scaletta restaurant in Milan, famed for its handmade pasta.

½ ounce dried porcini mushrooms

3 tablespoons olive oil

2 garlic cloves, finely chopped

handful fresh flat-leaf parsley, roughly chopped

2 large pieces drained sun-dried tomato in olive oil, sliced into thin strips

½ cup dry white wine

3½ cups thinly sliced cremini mushrooms

2 cups vegetable stock (page 19)

12 ounces spaghetti

sea salt and freshly ground black pepper

handful mixed chopped arugula and fresh flat-leaf parsley, to garnish

1 Put the porcini in a small bowl with ¾ cup warm water and let soak 15 to 20 minutes. In a fine sieve set over a bowl, drain the porcini and squeeze them with your hands to release as much liquid as possible; reserve the strained soaking liquid. Finely chop the porcini.

2 Heat the oil in a large skillet over medium heat. Add the garlic, parsley, sun-dried tomato strips, and porcini and sauté over low heat, stirring frequently, about 5 minutes.

3 Stir in the wine and simmer for a few minutes, until reduced by half. Stir in the cremini mushrooms and pour in the stock, then simmer, uncovered, 15 to 20 minutes, until the liquid reduces and the sauce is thick and rich.

4 Meanwhile, cook the pasta in boiling salted water about 10 minutes, until al dente, or tender but still firm to the bite.

5 Taste the mushroom sauce and adjust the seasoning, if necessary. Drain the pasta, reserving a little of the cooking liquid, and transfer it to a warm serving bowl. Add the mushroom sauce and toss well, thinning the sauce, if necessary, with some of the pasta cooking water.

6 Serve immediately, sprinkled liberally with the arugula and parsley.

Variation
To turn this everyday dish into a special-occasion treat, use mixed wild mushrooms, like fresh porcini (ceps), chanterelles, and morels. You can also stir in some heavy cream at the last minute for an extra-deluxe touch.

Pizzocheri della Valtellina Pasta Layer with Cabbage, Beans, and Potatoes   serves 6

This substantial dish from Lombardy is well suited to fending off the Alpine chill. Buckwheat pasta is also popular in this part of the world, as it is said to help stimulate the circulation.

FOR THE PASTA
2 cups buckwheat flour
1 cup all-purpose flour
3 eggs
7 tablespoons milk
pinch salt

FOR THE FILLING
7 ounces Idaho potatoes, peeled and cubed
sea salt and freshly ground black pepper
4 ounces each thin green beans and Brussels sprouts or cabbage
5 tablespoons unsalted butter
1 garlic clove, crushed
freshly grated nutmeg
handful fresh sage leaves
1 cup grated fontina cheese
¾ cup freshly grated Parmesan cheese

1 Make the pasta: Sift both the flours into a mound on a work surface and make a well in the middle. Beat the eggs together and pour into the well along with the milk, a little lukewarm water, and the salt. Mix together to a smooth dough, then let stand 10 minutes.

2 Roll out the dough into a paper-thin sheet. Roll it up from one long side and cut across into pieces about ½ inch wide; these will unroll into strips about 12 inches long.

3 Make the filling: cook the potatoes in boiling salted water until tender. Chop the cabbage, if using, and steam the other vegetables until tender.

4 Heat the butter in a saucepan over medium heat. Add the garlic and sauté gently until soft. Add the nutmeg, sage, and vegetables and stir to coat the vegetables in the melted butter. Season well with salt and pepper..

5 Cook the pasta in a large pot of boiling salted water about 6 minutes, until al dente, or just tender but still firm to the bite; drain well.

6 Put a layer of pasta in a large, warm serving dish followed by a layer of vegetables. Sprinkle with half of the cheeses. Repeat these layers. Serve hot.

Consiglio   As buckwheat pasta is hard to find, I've included the recipe for it. Buckwheat flour can be bought in most natural food stores.

Brandelli con Melanzane e Zucchini Brandelli with Eggplant and Zucchini Sauce   serves 4

Versions of this classic family dish are found all over southern Italy, where eggplants of all types are abundant.

7 ounces eggplant

sea salt and freshly ground black pepper

12 ounces brandelli (see Consiglio, below)

2 carrots

2 small zucchini

1 large onion

4 tablespoons olive oil

2 garlic cloves, crushed

1 tablespoon chopped fresh rosemary

7 tablespoons red wine

¾ cup freshly grated pecorino cheese

1 Peel the eggplant and chop the flesh into matchsticks. Put in a bowl and sprinkle with salt. Place a plate on top of the eggplant and weight down; set aside for 20 minutes.

2 Toward the end of this time, cook the pasta in a large pot of boiling salted water about 12 minutes, until al dente, or just tender but still firm to the bite.

3 While the pasta cooks, cut the carrots and zucchini into matchsticks and finely chop the onion. Rinse the eggplant matchsticks and pat dry.

4 Heat the oil in a saucepan over medium heat. Add the carrots, zucchini, and eggplant and fry until golden. Add the onion and fry until colored, then add the garlic and rosemary. Lower the heat and add the wine, with salt and pepper to taste. Cover and simmer 5 minutes.

5 Drain the pasta and toss it into the sauce. Serve sprinkled with the cheese.

Variation

Add a basic tomato sauce and some grated ricotta salata (see page 35) and you have something approximating the famous *pasta alla norma*.

Consiglio   **If the crinkled squares of brandelli are not available, use pappardelle or your favorite shape.**

Conchiglie Grandi Farcite Stuffed Giant Pasta Shells serves 2

These filled pasta shells are delicious on their own, or they can be served with a white béchamel sauce. Toasting the pine nuts makes them far tastier. You can toast a large batch at a time and store them in a jar in the refrigerator to keep them fresh.

12 giant pasta shells

salt and freshly ground black pepper

12 ounces broccoli florets

1/3 cup pine nuts

8 ounces Dolcelatte cheese

1 garlic clove, crushed

small handful finely snipped fresh chives

a little extra-virgin olive oil

freshly grated Parmesan cheese, to serve

1 Cook the pasta in a large pot of boiling salted water about 10 minutes, until al dente, or just tender but still firm to the bite.

2 While the pasta cooks, steam the broccoli about 8 minutes until tender.

3 Toast the pine nuts on a sheet of foil under a hot broiler, turning them frequently.

4 Put the broccoli, Dolcelatte, pine nuts, garlic, and chives in a bowl, season to taste with salt and pepper, and stir together.

5 Drain the pasta and toss it in a little oil to prevent the shells from sticking together. While still warm, stuff them with the broccoli mixture.

6 Place the stuffed pasta shells in a greased shallow baking dish, sprinkle the cheese over, and broil until bubbling. Serve immediately.

Variation
These large pasta shells suit a whole range of different stuffings — try roasted bell peppers and tomatoes or ham and mushrooms with cheese.

Conchiglie con Verdure Arrostite Conchiglie with Roasted Vegetables serves 4

Nothing could be simpler or more delicious than tossing freshly cooked pasta with roasted vegetables.

I red bell pepper, seeded and cut into ½-inch pieces

I yellow bell pepper, seeded and cut into ½-inch pieces

I small eggplant, roughly diced

2 zucchini, roughly diced

5 tablespoons extra-virgin olive oil

handful fresh flat-leaf parsley, chopped

I teaspoon dried oregano

sea salt and freshly ground black pepper

9 ounces cherry tomatoes, preferably vine-ripened, halved

2 garlic cloves, roughly chopped

12 ounces conchiglie (pasta shells; see page 42)

marjoram flowers or oregano flowers, to garnish (optional)

1 Heat the oven to 375°F. Rinse the prepared bell peppers, eggplant, and zucchini under running water. Drain, then lay the vegetables in a large roasting pan.

2 Pour 3 tablespoons of the oil over the vegetables and sprinkle with the parsley and oregano. Season to taste and stir well. Roast about 30 minutes, stirring 2 or 3 times.

3 Stir the tomatoes and garlic into the vegetable mixture and roast for 20 minutes longer, again stirring once or twice.

4 Meanwhile, cook the pasta in boiling salted water about 10 minutes, until al dente, or tender but still firm to the bite.

5 Drain the pasta and transfer it to a warm bowl. Add the roasted vegetables and the remaining oil and toss well.

6 Serve the pasta and vegetables hot in warm bowls, sprinkling each portion well with a few herb flowers, if you have them.

Variation
Try this dish with roast pumpkin, replacing the parsley and oregano with fresh sage leaves.

Rigatoni Casalinga Country-Style Rigatoni (with Zucchini, Red Onion, and Gorgonzola) serves 4

This rustic dish suits all sorts of additions and variations—it's the sort of thing you can heap leftover bacon, ham, or chicken into and get great results every time. Be creative.

12 ounces rigatoni (see page 41) or other pasta shape

sea salt and freshly ground black pepper

2 tender young zucchini

1 red onion

1 celery stalk

8 pitted olives

4 sun-dried tomatoes

4 ounces gorgonzola cheese

3 tablespoons olive oil

1 garlic clove, crushed

1 glass white wine

large handful fresh basil leaves

freshly grated Parmesan cheese, to serve

1 Cook the pasta in a large pot of boiling salted water about 10 minutes, until al dente, or just tender but still firm to the bite.

2 While the pasta cooks, cut the zucchini into julienne strips. Finely chop the onion and celery. Roughly chop the olives and sun-dried tomatoes. Cut the cheese into cubes. Steam the zucchini strips 2 minutes.

3 In a medium-size saucepan, heat the oil over medium heat. Add the onion and sauté about 5 minutes, until soft. Add the celery, garlic, and wine and simmer 6 minutes.

4 Add the zucchini strips, olives, sun-dried tomatoes, gorgonzola, basil, and salt and pepper to taste and stir together.

5 Drain the pasta and put it in a warm serving dish. Add the sauce and toss together. Adjust the seasoning to taste and serve immediately with Parmesan cheese.

Consiglio **The best sun-dried tomatoes are those without the seeds, because the seeds are bitter. Good sun-dried tomatoes should be slightly moist, sweet, and tender.**

Rigatoni con Aglio Arrostito, Peperoncino e Funghi
Rigatoni with Roasted Garlic, Chile, and Mushrooms   serves 4

Roasting garlic gives it an entirely different and much more complex flavor. Try different kinds of garlic and you will notice the subtle variations in the flavor.

2 whole garlic heads, plus 1 extra crushed garlic clove

2 tablespoons olive oil, plus extra to drizzle

1 fresh red chile

10 ounces portobello mushrooms

12 ounces rigatoni (see page 41)

sea salt and freshly ground black pepper

⅔ cup heavy cream

freshly grated Parmesan cheese, to serve

1 Heat the oven to 400°F. Slice the tops off the whole garlic heads and put the heads in a roasting pan. Drizzle with a little oil and roast 30 minutes, turning after 15 minutes; they will become golden and papery on the outside. Let cool slightly.

2 Finely chop the chile, discarding the seeds. Roughly chop the mushrooms. Heat the 2 tablespoons olive oil in a sauté pan. Add the mushrooms and sauté 8 minutes. Add the chile and the crushed garlic clove and sauté 4 minutes longer.

3 Meanwhile, cook the pasta in boiling salted water about 10 minutes, until al dente, or tender but still firm to the bite.

4 While the pasta is cooking, squeeze the roasted garlic cloves like toothpaste from a tube to extract the garlic pulp from each clove. Add the pulp to the mushroom mixture. Stir in the cream and add salt and pepper to taste.

5 Drain the pasta and pour the sauce over. Serve with the cheese.

Maccheroni con Broccoli in Tegame Macaroni with Broccoli and Cauliflower   serves 4

This is a southern Italian dish, full of vibrant flavors.

1¼ cups cauliflower florets, divided into small pieces

sea salt and freshly ground black pepper

1¼ cups broccoli florets, divided into small pieces

12 ounces short-cut macaroni

3 tablespoons olive oil

1 onion, finely chopped

3 tablespoons pine nuts

1 large pinch saffron powder, dissolved in 1 tablespoon warm water

1 tablespoon raisins (optional, see Consiglio, below)

2 tablespoons sun-dried tomato paste

4 canned anchovies in oil, chopped, plus extra, to serve (optional)

1 Cook the cauliflower in a large pot of boiling salted water 3 minutes. Add the broccoli and boil both together 2 minutes longer. Remove the vegetables from the pan with a large slotted spoon and set aside.

2 Add the pasta to the vegetable cooking water and bring back to a boil. Cook the pasta about 10 minutes, until al dente, or tender but still firm to the bite.

3 Meanwhile, heat the oil in a large skillet or pot over low to medium heat. Add the onion and sauté, stirring frequently, 2 to 3 minutes, until golden.

4 Add the pine nuts, the broccoli and cauliflower, the saffron water, raisins, if using, the sun-dried tomato paste, and a couple of ladlefuls of the pasta cooking water until the vegetable mixture has the consistency of a sauce. Finally add plenty of pepper and stir well.

5 Cook 1 to 2 minutes, then add the anchovies.

6 Drain the pasta and add it to the vegetable mixture. Toss well, then taste and adjust the seasoning, if necessary.

7 Serve the pasta immediately. You might like to add 1 or 2 whole anchovies on top of each serving.

Consiglio **If you are using the raisins, plump them up in the saffron water, but you might need to add another spoonful of water.**

Spaghetti alla Siracusana Spaghetti with Anchovies and Olives serves 4

Named after Syracuse, the great Sicilian port, the strong flavors of this dish are typical of the island's cuisine.

3 tablespoons olive oil

I large red bell pepper, seeded and chopped

I small eggplant, finely chopped

I onion, finely chopped

8 ripe Italian plum tomatoes, peeled, seeded, and finely chopped

2 garlic cloves, finely chopped

1/2 cup dry red wine

handful mixed fresh basil, flat-leaf parsley, and rosemary

sea salt and freshly ground black pepper

12 ounces dried spaghetti

2 ounces canned anchovies in oil, roughly chopped, plus extra to garnish

12 pitted black olives

I to 2 tablespoons salt-packed capers

1 Heat the oil in a saucepan and add all the chopped vegetables and the garlic. Cook gently, stirring frequently, 10 to 15 minutes, until the vegetables are soft.

2 Pour in the wine and 1/2 cup water. Add the herbs, and pepper to taste, and bring to a boil. Lower the heat and simmer, stirring occasionally, 10 to 15 minutes.

3 Meanwhile, cook the pasta in a large pot of boiling salted water about 10 minutes, until al dente, or just tender but still firm to the bite.

4 Add the chopped anchovies, the olives, and capers to the sauce. Heat through for a few minutes, then taste and adjust the seasoning, if necessary.

5 Drain the pasta and transfer to a warm bowl. Pour the sauce over the pasta, toss well, and serve garnished with the whole anchovies.

Chitarra con Sardine e Pane Grattati Chitarra with Sardines and Bread Crumbs serves 4

Chitarra is an interesting pasta that looks like spaghetti from a distance, but is actually square.

8 filleted fresh sardines

4 tablespoons olive oil

sea salt and freshly ground black pepper

14 ounces chitarra

2 garlic cloves, crushed

2 good handfuls fresh herbs, such as parsley, basil, and thyme, plus more flat-leaf parsley to garnish

I cup fresh white bread crumbs, toasted

1 Heat the broiler to medium. Brush the sardines with half the oil and season with salt and pepper. Broil for 8 minutes on each side, then set aside to cool.

2 Cook the pasta in a large pot of boiling salted water about 10 minutes, until al dente, or just tender but still firm to the bite.

3 Heat the remaining oil in a small sauté pan. Add the garlic and sauté gently, being careful not to let it color. Break up the sardines and add them, along with the herbs. Drain the pasta and toss it with the sardine mixture and the bread crumbs. Serve immediately in warm bowls, sprinkled with parsley.

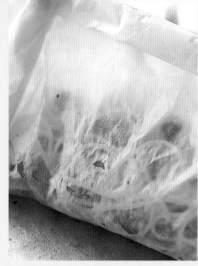

Pasta al Cartoccio con Tonno, Pomodoro e Patate Pasta in Paper with Tuna, Tomatoes, and Potatoes serves 4

Stunningly simple, this dish can be cooked ahead of time, is infinitely versatile, and is a great family favorite with my sisters and their children. Italians have cooked in paper for centuries, usually using fish. It speeds up cooking and seals in all the flavors, nutrients, and wonderful aromas.

9 ounces tuna steak, chopped into ¾-inch cubes
1 glass white wine
2 garlic cloves, finely chopped
grated zest of 1 lemon
2 sprigs fresh rosemary, broken into pieces
sea salt and freshly ground black pepper
8 new potatoes (preferably Italian), peeled and finely diced
12 ripe plum tomatoes (preferably Italian), seeded and roughly chopped
handful flat-leaf parsley, chopped, plus extra to serve
12 ounces spaghetti
2 tablespoons olive oil

1 Place the tuna in a bowl with the wine, garlic, lemon zest, and rosemary, and sprinkle with salt and pepper. Marinate 30 minutes. Heat the oven to 400°F.

2 Toward the end of the marinating time, cook the potatoes in boiling salted water 6 minutes, or until tender, and drain. Combine with the tomatoes and parsley, reserving some parsley for garnish.

3 At the same time, half-cook the pasta just over half the time suggested on the package; drain.

4 Heat the oil in a large skillet over medium-high heat until hot. Add the tuna with its marinade and fry very quickly 6 minutes. Combine with the pasta and the tomato mixture.

5 Lay out 4 pieces of parchment paper. Pile one-quarter of the mixture on each and fold the paper up loosely, like an envelope: Fold in the edges and then fold over the top carefully to seal completely.

6 Bake 7 minutes. Serve at once, slashing the paper packages at the table and sprinkling with more parsley.

zucchini and zucchini flowers

In a little oil, gently cook 4 thinly sliced tender, young zucchini with 1 finely chopped garlic clove, 2 tablespoons dry white wine, and salt and pepper 3 minutes until tender. Add a handful each of fresh flat-leaf parsley and mint, followed by 4 zucchini flowers, cut into strips. Mix this with the spaghetti and make into packages.

Anchovies, capers, and tomatoes

Thoroughly rinse 4 teaspoons salt-packed capers and finely chop. Add 8 drained and chopped best-quality, canned anchovies in oil, 8 seeded and chopped ripe plum tomatoes, a handful finely chopped fresh flat-leaf parsley, and 1 finely chopped garlic clove. Season with pepper only and mix well. Mix this with the spaghetti and make into packages.

Fava beans, red onions, mint, and pecorino

Sauté 2 sliced red onions in a little butter. Add 3 cups shelled fresh fava beans with a handful of chopped fresh mint, 1 chopped garlic clove, and salt and pepper to taste. Cook, stirring frequently, until the beans are just tender. Let cool, then add ⅔ cup freshly grated pecorino cheese (preferably Romano). Mix this with the spaghetti and make into packages.

Tomatoes, olives, parsley, and garlic

Mix together 8 seeded and chopped ripe plum tomatoes, 12 pitted and chopped fruity black olives, 2 finely chopped garlic cloves, a handful chopped fresh flat-leaf parsley, and salt and pepper to taste. Mix this with the spaghetti and make into packages.

Farfalle con Pollo e Pomodorini Farfalle with Chicken and Cherry Tomatoes serves 4

I have made this using leftover roast turkey (cooking only enough to warm through) to great acclaim.

12 ounces skinless, boneless chicken breast halves, cut into bite-size pieces

4 tablespoons Italian dry vermouth

2 teaspoons chopped fresh rosemary, plus 4 fresh rosemary sprigs, to garnish

sea salt and freshly ground black pepper

I tablespoon olive oil

I onion, finely chopped

3 ounces Italian salami, diced

10 ounces dried farfalle (see page 45)

I tablespoon balsamic vinegar

one 14-ounce can Italian cherry tomatoes

good pinch crushed dried red chiles

1 Put the chicken pieces in a large bowl, pour the dry vermouth over, and sprinkle with half the chopped rosemary, and salt and pepper to taste; stir well and set aside.

2 Heat the oil in a large saucepan over medium heat. Add the onion and salami and fry, stirring frequently, about 5 minutes.

3 Meanwhile, cook the pasta in a large pot of boiling salted water about 10 minutes, until al dente, or just tender but still firm to the bite.

4 Add the chicken and vermouth to the onion and salami, increase the heat to high and fry 3 minutes, or until the chicken is white on all sides. Sprinkle the vinegar over the chicken. Add the cherry tomatoes and dried chiles, stir well, and simmer a few minutes longer. Taste the sauce and adjust the seasoning, if necessary.

5 Drain the pasta and add it to the sauce. Add the remaining chopped rosemary and toss to mix the pasta and sauce together. Serve immediately, in warm bowls, garnished with rosemary sprigs.

Variation
Instead of chicken breast, try well-trimmed chicken livers.

Penne alla Rusticana Penne with Chicken, Broccoli, and Cheese   serves 4

Quick to prepare and easy to cook, this colorful dish is full of flavor.

¾ **cup broccoli florets, divided into tiny pieces**

sea salt and freshly ground black pepper

4 tablespoons unsalted butter

2 skinless, boneless chicken breast halves, cut into thin strips

2 garlic cloves, crushed

14 ounces dried penne (see page 39)

½ **cup dry white wine**

1 cup heavy cream

¾ **cup rinded gorgonzola cheese, finely diced**

freshly grated Parmesan cheese, to serve

1 Plunge the broccoli into a saucepan of boiling salted water. Bring back to a boil and boil 2 minutes, then drain and refresh in cold water. Shake well to remove excess water and set aside to drain completely.

2 Melt the butter in a large pot over medium heat. Add the chicken and garlic with salt and pepper to taste, stir well, and fry 3 minutes, or until the chicken becomes white.

3 Meanwhile, cook the pasta in a large pot of boiling salted water about 10 minutes, until al dente, or just tender but still firm to the bite.

4 Pour the wine and cream over the chicken mixture in the pan and stir to mix, then simmer, stirring occasionally, about 5 minutes, until the sauce reduces and thickens. Add the broccoli, increase the heat, and toss to heat through. Taste and adjust the seasoning, if necessary.

5 Drain the pasta and add it to the sauce. Add the gorgonzola and toss well. Serve with the Parmesan.

Variation

For an even more substantial dish, add sliced pancetta and chopped fresh sage with the chicken.

Eliche con Salsiccia e Radicchio Eliche with Sausage and Radicchio serves 4

This robust and hearty flavor combination is from Treviso in the north, where lots of radicchio is grown. Eliche are the pasta spirals that look more like screw-threads or propellers than fusilli.

2 tablespoons olive oil

I onion, finely chopped

7 ounces Italian pure pork sausage

¾ cup tomato puree

6 tablespoons dry white wine

sea salt and freshly ground black pepper

12 ounces dried eliche

2 ounces radicchio leaves

1 Heat the oil in a large, deep pot over low heat. Add the onion and sauté, stirring frequently, about 5 minutes, until soft.

2 Cut the sausage into bite-size chunks and add it to the pan. Stir to mix with the oil and onion and continue to fry the mixture, increasing the heat, if necessary, until the sausage is brown all over.

3 Stir in the tomato puree, then sprinkle in the wine and season to taste with salt and pepper. Simmer over low heat, uncovered, stirring occasionally, 10 to 12 minutes.

4 Meanwhile, cook the pasta in a large pot of boiling salted water about 10 minutes, until al dente, or just tender but still firm to the bite.

5 Just before draining the pasta, add 1 or 2 ladlefuls of the cooking water to the sausage sauce and stir well. Taste the sauce and adjust the seasoning, if necessary. Thinly slice the radicchio leaves.

6 Drain the pasta and add it to the pan of sausage sauce. Add the radicchio and toss well to combine. Serve immediately.

Variation
If you can't find Italian sausages, use Cumberland, Toulouse, or any spicy sausage.

Bucatini alla Posillipo Bucatini with Sausage and Pancetta   serves 4

Named after a restaurant in Palermo, Sicily, this is a rich and satisfying dish. It hardly needs grated Parmesan cheese as an accompaniment, but you can hand some around in a separate bowl, if you wish.

4 ounces pork sausage meat
one 14-ounce can Italian plum tomatoes
1 tablespoon olive oil
1 garlic clove, crushed
4 ounces sliced pancetta or bacon, roughly chopped
handful chopped fresh flat-leaf parsley
sea salt and freshly ground black pepper
14 ounces dried bucatini (see page 40)
4 to 5 tablespoons heavy cream
2 egg yolks

1 Remove any skin from the sausage meat and break the meat up roughly with a knife. Puree the tomatoes in a food processor or blender.

2 Heat the oil in a medium saucepan over low heat. Add the garlic and sauté 1 to 2 minutes. Remove and discard the garlic.

3 Increase the heat to medium, add the sausage meat and pancetta, and sauté 3 to 4 minutes. Stir constantly with a wooden spoon to break up the sausage meat—it will become brown and look crumbly.

4 Add the tomatoes to the pan, along with half the parsley, and salt and pepper to taste. Stir well and bring to a boil, scraping up any browned bits stuck to the bottom of the pan. Lower the heat, cover, and simmer 20 minutes, stirring from time to time. Taste and adjust the seasoning, if necessary.

5 Meanwhile, cook the pasta in a large pot of boiling salted water about 10 minutes, until al dente, or tender but still firm to the bite.

6 Put the cream, egg yolks, and salt and pepper to taste in a large warm bowl and mix with a fork. As soon as the pasta is cooked, drain it well and add it to the cream mixture. Toss until the pasta is coated, then pour the sausage meat sauce over the pasta and toss again.

7 Serve immediately in warm bowls, sprinkled with the remaining parsley.

Consiglio   To save time pureeing the tomatoes, use tomato puree. For authenticity, buy *salsiccia a metro*, a pure pork sausage sold by the yard at Italian delicatessens. Bucatini is a long, hollow pasta that looks like firm drinking straws; spaghetti works equally well.

Tagliatelle verdi al Sugo di Piselli Green Tagliatelle with Fresh Pea Sauce   serves 4

Here tagliatelle is used, but other pasta shapes—say, farfalle—will work just as well. The use of pasta verde (spinach pasta) is very much a northern Italian thing.

I tablespoon olive oil

5 or 6 bacon slices, cut into strips

one 14½-ounce can crushed Italian plum tomatoes

sea salt and freshly ground black pepper

12 ounces dried tagliatelle verde

1½ cups shelled peas, preferably fresh or frozen in a pinch

¼ cup mascarpone cheese

a few fresh basil leaves, torn, plus extra whole leaves to garnish

freshly grated Parmesan cheese, to serve

1 Heat the oil in a medium-size saucepan over low heat. Add the bacon and sauté, stirring frequently, 5 to 7 minutes.

2 Add the tomatoes and 4 tablespoons water and season to taste with salt and pepper. Bring to a boil, lower the heat, cover, and simmer slowly about 15 minutes, stirring from time to time.

3 Meanwhile, cook the pasta in a large pot of boiling salted water about 10 minutes, until al dente, or. tender but still firm to the bite.

4 Add the peas to the tomato sauce, stir well to mix, and bring to a boil. Cover the pan and cook 5 to 8 minutes, until the peas are tender and the sauce is very thick. Taste and adjust the seasoning, if necessary.

5 Turn off the heat under the pan and stir in the mascarpone and torn basil leaves. Cover the pan and let stand 1 to 2 minutes.

6 Drain the pasta and transfer it to a warm serving bowl. Pour the sauce over the pasta and toss well.

7 Serve immediately, garnished with basil leaves, and hand around some grated Parmesan separately.

Consiglio **This sauce is usually served with plain white pasta. The red, green, and white make it *tricolore*, the colors of the Italian flag.**

5

leggero e sano
light & healthy

Pasta itself is basically high in complex carbohydrates and low in fat, and it is only the sauces that might introduce high levels of fats. What is more, the primary fat in pasta sauces tends to be healthy olive oil. You can also, as in this chapter, make a point of including foods that contain plant chemicals that are positively good for you, like broccoli and—of course—tomatoes, both of which are believed to help protect against cancer and heart disease.

Spaghetti con Pomodorini Spaghetti with Tiny Tomatoes   serves 2

The tomato is at the heart of many pasta sauces, and it is perhaps no coincidence as it is now known that the lycopenes in which it is so rich are potent agents against heart disease and many types of cancer. Moreover, these powers seem to get even stronger when the tomato is cooked. I always try to buy Italian tomatoes, as they seem to be full of sunshine and this gives them much more flavor than domestic ones.

I pound cherry tomatoes

3 large garlic cloves, cut into slivers

sea salt and freshly ground black pepper

7 ounces spaghetti

I small hot red chile pepper, seeded and chopped (optional)

I tablespoon olive oil for the chile, if necessary

handful fresh basil, torn

2 tablespoons extra-virgin olive oil

freshly grated Parmesan cheese, to serve

1 Heat the oven to 300°F. Cut the tomatoes in half and put them on a baking sheet. Place a sliver of garlic on top of each, followed by a sprinkling of salt. Bake 1 1/4 hours, until dry but still squashy.

2 Cook the pasta in a large pot of boiling salted water for about 10 minutes, until al dente, or just tender but still firm to the bite. If using the chile, fry it in olive oil just long enough to color it, then remove it from the heat.

3 Drain the pasta and stir in the tomatoes, chile, if using, basil, and extra-virgin olive oil, with salt and pepper to taste.

4 Serve sprinkled with the cheese.

Consiglio The last person to be served is the luckiest, as they get the most sauce.

Penne con Pomodori Gratinati Penne with Gratinéed Tomatoes serves 4

The region of **Campania** has been blessed with all of the proper elements for growing fruit and vegetables of unique quality—rich volcanic soil, a profusion of bright sunlight, and a gentle climate—and the diet of the region relies heavily on them. The goodness of Campania's **San Marzano** tomato, a thick-fleshed cooking tomato, is hailed around the world. When I am teaching, I also refer to this tomato as the one "with shoulders," meaning it has an attitude, because it has such a unique flavor.

3 tablespoons olive oil

4 ounces salt-packed capers

2 garlic cloves

16 large plum tomatoes, cored, cut in half lengthwise, and seeded

¼ cup dry bread crumbs

12 ounces penne (see page 39)

sea salt and freshly ground black pepper

2 tablespoons fine, fruity extra-virgin olive oil

handful fresh basil leaves, torn

freshly grated **Parmesan** cheese, to serve

1 Heat the oven to 300°F and grease two 13-x-9-inch baking sheets with a little of the olive oil.

2 Soak the capers in three changes of cold water to remove the salt; drain and pat them dry with paper towels.

3 Combine the capers and garlic on a cutting board and finely chop them together.

4 Arrange the tomatoes, cut side up, on the baking sheets. Sprinkle the caper mixture over the tomatoes, drizzle with the remaining olive oil, and then sprinkle with the bread crumbs. Roast 45 minutes, or until the tomatoes are very soft but still hold their shape.

5 Cook the pasta in a large pot of boiling salted water about 10 minutes, until al dente, or just tender, but still firm to the bite. Drain and transfer the pasta to a large, warm serving bowl. Spoon the tomato mixture and the extra-virgin olive oil over, then sprinkle with some pepper and the basil.

6 Serve immediately in warm bowls. Pass a bowl of cheese around to sprinkle on top.

Variation
Instead of the capers, add piquancy with a small can of anchovy fillets in oil, drained. Either way, a chopped seeded chile also adds a bit of zing.

Penne con Salsa di Melanzane Penne with Eggplant Sauce serves 4

1 medium eggplant

sea salt and freshly ground black pepper

3 tablespoons olive oil

4 tablespoons red wine

1 small onion, finely chopped

one 14½-ounce can crushed tomatoes

1 garlic clove, crushed

12 ounces penne (see page 39)

2 tablespoons heavy cream

1 tablespoon finely chopped fresh oregano

freshly grated Parmesan cheese, to serve (optional)

1 Cut the eggplant into medium-size cubes. Sprinkle with salt, place in a bowl, cover, and weight down; let sit 15 minutes. (This helps break down the cells so the eggplant absorbs less oil during cooking, and also helps draw out bitterness you might find in older specimens.) Rinse the eggplant and pat dry.

2 Heat the oil in a skillet over medium-high heat. Add the eggplant cubes and fry 5 minutes, until golden. Add the wine and simmer 15 minutes.

3 Add the onion and tomatoes to the eggplant. Bring to a boil, then lower the heat and simmer 10 minutes. Add the garlic.

4 While the sauce is simmering, cook the pasta in a large pot of boiling salted water about 10 minutes, until al dente, or just tender, but still firm to the bite.

5 Just before serving, stir the cream and oregano into the sauce. Drain the pasta and toss it with the sauce. Serve at once, with cheese, if you want.

Garganelli con Verdure di Stagione Garganelli with Spring Vegetables serves 4

3 tablespoons olive oil

2 carrots, diced

1 celery stalk, diced

1 garlic clove, peeled and crushed

1 small red onion, chopped

2 small zucchini, diced

¾ cup freshly shelled peas

2 ripe tomatoes, diced

1 teaspoon fresh thyme leaves

handful fresh basil leaves, torn

handful fresh flat-leaf parsley, chopped

sea salt and freshly ground black pepper

12 ounces garganelli (ridged, pointed tubes; see page 138)

2 tablespoons heavy cream

freshly grated Parmesan cheese

1 Heat the oil in a deep sauté pan over low heat. Add the carrots, celery, garlic, onion, zucchini, and peas and sauté, stirring frequently, 10 minutes, or until tender. Add the tomatoes, cover, and simmer over low heat about 6 minutes, then add the herbs and salt and pepper to taste.

2 Cook the pasta in a large pot of boiling salted water 7 to 10 minutes, until al dente, or just tender but still firm to the bite.

3 Drain the pasta and toss it with the vegetable sauce, adding the cream, and cheese to taste. Serve immediately.

Conchiglie con Salsa di Finocchio e Pomodoro
Conchiglie with Fennel and Tomato Sauce   serves 4

Fennel is said to cleanse the system, especially the liver.

2 fennel bulbs

3 tablespoons olive oil

I garlic clove

one 14½-ounce can crushed tomatoes

grated zest of I unwaxed lemon

handful fresh mint leaves, chopped

12 ounces conchiglie (pasta shells; see page 42)

sea salt and freshly ground black pepper

freshly grated Parmesan cheese, to serve

1 Heat the oven to 400°F.

2 Remove the fennel's tough outer leaves and tough core, and wash well. Cut into pieces and steam or cook in boiling water 7 to 8 minutes until tender. Transfer to a roasting pan and drizzle I tablespoon of the oil over. Roast 15 minutes, or until golden.

3 Meanwhile, crush the garlic. Heat the remaining oil in a saucepan over medium heat. Add the garlic and sauté until soft. Add the tomatoes, lemon zest, and mint and simmer slowly 25 minutes.

4 Toward the end of this time, cook the pasta in a large pot of boiling salted water about 10 minutes, until al dente or just tender but still firm to the bite.

5 Chop the fennel into small pieces and add it to the sauce. Season well with salt and pepper and heat slowly.

6 Drain the pasta and toss it with the sauce. Serve hot, with plenty of cheese.

Spaghetti con Castagne e Salvia Spaghetti with Chestnuts and Sage   **serves 4**

1 pound, 2 ounces fresh chestnuts, with a slit on each one

2 tablespoons olive oil

2 garlic cloves, roughly chopped

handful fresh flat-leaf parsley, chopped

generous handful fresh sage leaves, roughly chopped

1 1/4 cups canned crushed tomatoes

sea salt and freshly ground black pepper

12 ounces spaghetti

freshly grated Parmesan cheese, to serve (optional)

1 Heat the oven to 400°F. Place the chestnuts in a medium-size saucepan with enough water to cover. Bring to a boil and boil 10 minutes. Drain, place on a baking sheet, and roast 35 minutes. Leave to cool, then peel and chop.

2 Heat the oil in a medium-size saucepan over low heat. Add the garlic, parsley, sage, and tomatoes and simmer very slowly, covered, 15 minutes. Add the chestnuts, season with salt and pepper, and simmer 10 minutes longer.

3 Meanwhile, cook the pasta in a large pot of boiling salted water about 10 minutes, until al dente, or just tender but still firm to the bite.

4 Adjust the seasoning of the sauce, then drain the pasta and stir it into the sauce, mixing well. Serve immediately, with cheese, if you wish.

Pasta Vesuvio Pasta Vesuvius   **serves 4**

This is obviously named for its hot and fiery flavor. If you don't like hot food, it is still very delicious without the chile. Use light cream for a lighter dish and mascarpone for authenticity.

4 tomatoes

7 ounces fettuccine

sea salt and freshly ground black pepper

1 ounce pitted black or green olives

2 tablespoons capers

1 tablespoon olive oil

1 garlic clove, crushed

1/2 dried chile, seeded and chopped

handful fresh flat-leaf parsley, finely chopped, plus more to garnish

handful fresh mint leaves, finely chopped, plus more whole sprigs to garnish

2 tablespoons mascarpone cheese or light cream

2 teaspoons freshly grated Parmesan cheese

1 Put the tomatoes in a bowl, cover with boiling water, and let sit about 40 seconds then plunge into cold water. Using a sharp knife, peel off the skins and chop the flesh, discarding the seeds.

2 Cook the pasta in a large pot of boiling salted water about 10 minutes, until al dente, or just tender but still firm to the bite.

3 Meanwhile, finely chop the olives and capers. Heat the oil in a saucepan over medium heat. Add the garlic and sauté until soft. Add the olives, capers, tomatoes, chile, parsley, and mint and sauté about 5 minutes. Add the mascarpone cheese with salt and pepper to taste.

4 Drain the pasta, add it to the pan, and toss it together with the Parmesan cheese. Garnish with parsley and sprigs of mint.

Consiglio   **For a special occasion, when you are not so concerned with fat and calories, add a little heavy cream to the sauce at the end of step 3.**

Trenette alla Genovese Trenette with Pesto, Green Beans, and Potatoes   serves 2

In Liguria, it is traditional to serve pesto with trenette, thin green beans, and diced potatoes. The ingredients for making pesto are expensive, so the beans and potatoes are added to help make the pesto go further. The people of Genoa are notoriously frugal.

2 potatoes (about 9 ounces)

3½ ounces thin green beans

sea salt and freshly ground black pepper

12 ounces dried trenette (see below)

FOR THE PESTO

very generous handful fresh basil leaves

2 garlic cloves, thinly sliced

1½ tablespoons pine nuts

3 tablespoons freshly grated Parmesan cheese, plus extra, to serve

2 tablespoons freshly grated pecorino cheese

4 tablespoons extra-virgin olive oil

sea salt

1 First make the pesto: Put the basil leaves, garlic, pine nuts, and cheeses in a blender or food processor and process about 5 seconds. Add half of the oil and a pinch of salt and process 5 seconds longer. Stop the machine, remove the lid, and scrape down the side of the bowl. Add the remaining oil and process 5 to 10 seconds longer.

2 Cut the potatoes in half lengthwise, then cut each half across into ¼-inch-thick slices. Cut the beans into ¾-inch pieces. Plunge the potatoes and beans into a large pot of boiling salted water and boil, uncovered, 5 minutes.

3 Add the pasta, bring the water back to a boil, stir well, and cook 5 to 7 minutes, until the pasta is al dente, or just tender but still firm to the bite.

4 Meanwhile, put the pesto in a large bowl, add 3 to 4 tablespoons of the pasta cooking water, and stir well.

5 Drain the pasta and vegetables, add them to the pesto, and toss well. Serve immediately on warm plates with extra grated cheeses handed around separately.

Consiglio **Don't worry if the potatoes break up during cooking, as this will add to the creaminess of the finished dish.**

The pesto can be made up to 2 or 3 days in advance and kept in a bowl in the refrigerator until needed. Pour a thin layer of olive oil over the top and cover the bowl lightly with plastic wrap before refrigerating.

Trenette is the traditional Ligurian pasta that is served with pesto, but if you find it difficult to obtain you can use bavette or linguine instead. The two-colored paglia e fieno ("straw and hay") is another good choice.

Pasta con Calabrese Pasta with Broccoli   serves 2

Some of the best broccoli is grown in the south of Italy, hence its other name, *calabrese*—from Calabria. Here I've combined it with pasta and homemade toasted bread crumbs. To make the bread crumbs, spread day-old bread crumbs on a baking sheet and bake in an oven preheated to 375°F, stirring frequently, about 10 minutes, until golden.

7 ounces ditali (short macaroni)
sea salt and freshly ground black pepper
13 ounces broccoli
3 or 4 bay leaves
2 ounces pitted green olives
2 tablespoons olive oil
1 garlic clove, finely chopped
⅓ cup finely ground blanched almonds
3 tablespoons freshly toasted bread crumbs (see above)
extra-virgin olive oil, to serve
freshly grated Parmesan cheese, to serve

1 Cook the pasta in a large pot of boiling salted water about 10 minutes, until al dente, or just tender but still firm to the bite.

2 While the pasta is cooking, cut the broccoli into florets and steam them with the bay leaves about 6 minutes, until tender.

3 While the pasta and broccoli are cooking, finely chop the olives. Heat the olive oil and garlic in a frying pan, add the olives and ground almonds, and heat very gently, adding a tablespoon of water.

4 Drain the cooked pasta, toss in the broccoli, olive mixture, and bread crumbs, and mix well. Drizzle over some extra-virgin olive oil and serve with Parmesan cheese.

Consiglio Broccoli is one of the healthiest of vegetables. It is high in fiber, packed full of the antioxidant beta-carotene and vitamin C, which help fight heart disease and cancer, and "phytochemicals" called glucosinolates, which also help protect against a range of cancers by stimulating the body's natural defenses.

Tearing a fresh bay leaf helps release its aroma and flavor.

Orecchiette con Rucola Orecchiette with Arugula serves 4

This hearty dish is from Puglia, in the southeast of Italy.

3 tablespoons olive oil
I small onion, finely chopped
½ cups crushed plum
tomatoes or tomato puree
½ teaspoon dried oregano
pinch of chile flakes
about 2 tablespoons white wine
(optional)
sea salt and freshly ground black
pepper
12 ounces dried orecchiette
(see page 102)
2 garlic cloves, finely chopped
5 ounces arugula leaves, stalks
removed, leaves shredded
3 tablespoons ricotta
freshly grated pecorino cheese,
to serve

1 Heat I tablespoon of the oil in a medium-size saucepan over medium heat. Add half of the onion and sauté, stirring frequently, about 5 minutes, until soft. Add the tomatoes, oregano, and chile flakes. Pour in the wine, if using, and add a little salt and pepper to taste. Cover the pan and simmer about 15 minutes, stirring occasionally.

2 Meanwhile, cook the pasta in a large pot of boiling salted water about 15 minutes, until al dente, or just tender but still firm to the bite.

3 Heat the remaining oil in a large saucepan. Add the remaining onion and the garlic and fry 2 to 3 minutes, stirring occasionally. Add the arugula, toss over the heat about 2 minutes, until it wilts, then stir in the tomato sauce and the ricotta.

4 Drain the pasta, add it to the pan of sauce, and toss to mix. Taste and adjust the seasoning, if necessary. Serve immediately in warm bowls with the pecorino handed around separately.

Seven deadly sins (wild herbs) **Mix together
a small handful each of fresh parsley, basil, thyme,
rosemary, sage, oregano, and marjoram and finely chop
them all. Stir all the chopped herbs into the pasta instead
of the arugula, omitting the dried oregano.**

Sun-dried tomatoes and radicchio **Cut about
10 drained sun-dried tomatoes in oil into strips and shred
a large head of radicchio, preferably Treviso. Stir both of
these into the pasta instead of the arugula.**

Baby spinach and blue cheese **Cut 7 ounces
gorgonzola picante into small cubes. Stir these and
about 12 ounces of young spinach leaves into the pasta
instead of the arugula, and omitting the ricotta.**

Eggplant **Cut a large eggplant into small cubes and
salt and rinse these as described on page 87. Stir them
into the pasta instead of the arugula.**

Linguine con Vongole e Cime di Rape Linguine with Fresh Clams and Turnip Greens serves 4

Humble turnip greens have long been popular in Italy, and they are beginning to be rediscovered abroad. If you can't find them, do ask your grocer or supermarket to get them in. It's what I have done, and now they sell them to all comers. Linguine are the noodles that are oval in section, looking a bit like a flattened spaghetti.

1 ½ **pounds live Venus clams or** *vongole verace*

a little all-purpose flour

2 **tablespoons olive oil**

2 **leeks, thinly sliced**

2 **fresh bay leaves**

1 **garlic clove, crushed**

7 **ounces dry white wine**

sea salt and freshly ground black pepper

12 **ounces linguine**

12 ounces turnip greens (*cime di rape*), finely chopped

3 **tablespoons roughly chopped fresh flat-leaf parsley**

1 Keep the clams submerged in water, with a little flour added to the water (which helps plump them up and purge them of any dirt). Discard any open ones that don't close when tapped.

2 Heat the oil in a large saucepan over high heat. Add the leeks and bay leaves and sauté until the leeks have some color. Add the garlic and wine, salt and pepper to taste, and the drained clams. Cover and cook over medium-high heat about 6 minutes, until all the clams open. Discard any clams that don't open.

3 At the same time, cook the linguine in a large pot of boiling salted water about 10 minutes, until al dente, or just tender but still firm to the bite. Drain.

4 Remove the lid from the clam pan and throw in the turnip greens and stir. Add the drained linguine and the parsley. Mix well, adjust the seasoning, and serve immediately.

Variation
If you can't find turnip greens, use chard or spinach.

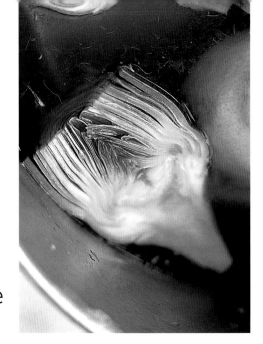

Penne ai Gamberi e Carciofi Penne with Shrimp and Artichokes serves 4

This is a good dish to make in late spring or early summer, when green-purple baby artichokes appear in shops and market stalls. I have a great fondness for artichokes; they taste so wonderful and are really good for your liver as a cleanser. All Italians are obsessed with their livers, claiming it to be the "happy organ."

juice of 1 lemon
4 baby globe artichokes, preferably with good long stalks
3 tablespoons olive oil
2 garlic cloves, crushed
handful fresh mint leaves, chopped
handful fresh flat-leaf parsley, chopped
sea salt and freshly ground black pepper
12 ounces dried penne (see page 39)
16 shelled jumbo shrimp, each cut into 2 or 3 pieces
2 tablespoons fruity, fine extra-virgin olive oil

1 Have ready a pan of cold water to which you have added the lemon juice. To prepare the artichokes, cut off the artichoke stalks, if any, and cut across the tops of the leaves. Peel off and discard any tough or discolored outer leaves. Cut the artichokes lengthwise into quarters and remove the hairy chokes from their centers. Put the pieces of artichoke in the pan of acidulated water to help prevent them from discoloring. Bring to a boil and simmer gently for about 10 minutes.

2 Drain the artichokes and pat them dry. Heat the olive oil in a nonstick skillet over low heat and add the artichokes, the garlic, and half of the mint and parsley. Season with plenty of salt and pepper. Sauté, stirring frequently, about 3 to 4 minutes, until the artichokes are just tender.

3 Meanwhile, cook the pasta in a large pot of boiling salted water until al dente, or just tender, but still firm to the bite.

4 Add the shrimp to the artichokes, stir well to mix, then heat through gently for 2 minutes.

5 Drain the pasta and transfer it to a warm bowl. Dress with the extra-virgin olive oil, spoon the artichoke mixture over the pasta, and toss to combine.

6 Serve immediately, sprinkled with the remaining mint and parsley.

Orecchiette con Acciughe e Broccoli Orecchiette with Anchovies and Broccoli serves 4

With its robust flavors, this dish is typical of Puglia, southern Italy, and, in fact, Sicily. Anchovies, pine nuts, garlic, and pecorino cheese are all very popular ingredients there. Serve with crusty bread to mop up the juices.

12 ounces broccoli florets

sea salt and freshly ground black pepper

2 tablespoons pine nuts

12 ounces dried orecchiette (see below)

2 tablespoons olive oil

I small red onion, thinly sliced

2-ounce jar of anchovies in olive oil, drained

I garlic clove crushed

2 tablespoons freshly grated pecorino cheese

1 Divide the broccoli florets into small pieces and cut off the stems. If the stems are large, chop or slice them. Cook the broccoli florets and stems in a saucepan of boiling salted water 2 minutes, then drain and refresh them in cold water; drain on paper towels.

2 Put the pine nuts in a dry nonstick skillet over low to medium heat 1 to 2 minutes, until the nuts are lightly toasted; remove from the pan and set aside.

3 Cook the pasta in a large pot of boiling salted water about 10 minutes until al dente, or just tender, but still firm to the bite.

4 Meanwhile, heat the oil in a frying pan, add the onion, and fry gently, stirring frequently, about 5 minutes, until softened. Add the anchovies, followed by the garlic, and cook over medium heat until the anchovies break down to a paste. Add the broccoli and plenty of pepper and toss over the heat 1 or 2 minutes, until the broccoli is hot. Taste and adjust the seasoning.

5 Drain the pasta and transfer it to a warm bowl. Add the broccoli mixture and grated pecorino, and toss well to combine. Sprinkle with the pine nuts and serve immediately in warm bowls.

Variation
Sometimes I add 4 diced fresh tomatoes to this mixture. You can also add cooked borlotti beans with chopped parsley.

Consiglio Orecchiette (little ears) from Puglia are a special type of pasta with a chewy texture. You can get them in Italian delis, or use conchiglie instead.

Bucatini alle Sarde e Finocchio Bucatini with Sardines and Fennel   serves 4

This tasty and substantial dish is obviously southern in origin.

13 ounces bucatini (see page 40)

FOR THE SAUCE
3 tablespoons olive oil
I onion, finely chopped
2 garlic cloves, peeled and crushed
generous handful fennel fronds, finely chopped
one 14½-ounce can crushed tomatoes
I teaspoon currants
⅔ cup pine nuts
I teaspoon dried chile flakes
sea salt
18 ounces fresh sardine fillets, rinsed

FOR THE PASTA TOPPING
I cup fresh white bread crumbs
2 tablespoons olive oil
4 ripe tomatoes, seeded and chopped
I garlic clove, peeled and crushed
dried chile flakes
handful fresh flat-leaf parsley, chopped

I First make the sauce: Heat the oil over medium heat. Add the onion and garlic and sauté until they are soft. Add the fennel fronds, tomatoes, currants, pine nuts, chile flakes, and a little salt. Simmer, stirring from time to time, 30 minutes.

2 Add the sardine fillets and cook 12 minutes—they will break up while cooking.

3 Meanwhile, make the pasta topping. Toast the bread crumbs in a skillet, mixing in the oil, tomatoes, garlic, a little salt, and a pinch of chile flakes. Stir constantly, without letting the bread crumbs burn, until they are a nice amber color and crunchy to the bite. Sprinkle the parsley over the mixture.

4 Cook the pasta in a large pot of boiling salted water until al dente, or just tender but still firm to the bite.

5 Reserving a ladleful of the cooking water, drain the pasta. Pour half of the sauce into the pasta pot. Add the pasta and stir to coat completely. Pour into a serving dish and cover with the rest of the sauce, adding the reserved cooking water if needed to yield enough sauce. Serve immediately, topped with the bread crumb mixture.

Variation
If you can't get fennel with green fronds attached, use fresh dill. Although the taste doesn't really compare, if you make this dish with canned sardines, it still makes a very nice supper.

Consiglio Instead of squid and peas, you could add chunks of roasted vegetables such as zucchini, bell peppers or eggplant to the tomato sauce, or Bolognese sauce (page 134) can be used instead of tomato sauce.

Pasticciata con Calamari e Piselli
Pasta Pie with Squid and Peas   serves 4 to 6

This is an excellent supper dish for all the family; children absolutely love it. Most of the ingredients will probably already be in your pantry or refrigerator, so more basic versions of it make good "stand-by" meals—you could, for example, substitute canned tuna for the squid. Pasticciata can be made with or without pastry crusts. Naturally here we make it without to keep it light and healthy.

12 ounces dried conchiglie (pasta shells; see page 42) or rigatoni (see page 41)

about 6 medium-sized squid, cleaned

grated zest and juice of 1 unwaxed lemon

1 ½ cups fresh shelled peas

2 tablespoons dry bread crumbs

FOR THE TOMATO SAUCE
2 tablespoons olive oil
1 small onion, finely chopped
one 14½-ounce can crushed Italian plum tomatoes
1 tablespoon sun-dried tomato paste
handful mixed herbs, such as sage, thyme, rosemary, and flat-leaf parsley, chopped
sea salt and freshly ground black pepper

FOR THE WHITE SAUCE
2 tablespoons unsalted butter
2 tablespoons Italian 00-grade flour (see page 8) or all-purpose flour
2½ cups skim milk
1 egg

1 First make the tomato sauce: Heat the oil in a large saucepan, add the onion and cook over gentle heat, stirring, until softened. Stir in the tomatoes, then fill the empty can with water and add it to the tomato mixture along with the tomato paste and herbs, and salt and pepper to taste. Simmer 20 minutes.

2 Meanwhile, preheat the oven to 375°F. Cook the pasta in a large pot of boiling salted water, until al dente, or just tender but still firm to the bite.

3 While the pasta is cooking, make the white sauce: Melt the butter in a pan, add the flour and cook, stirring, 1 minute. A little at a time, add the milk, whisking well after each addition. Bring to a boil and cook, stirring, until the sauce is smooth and thick. Season to taste, then remove the pan from the heat and set aside.

4 Chop the squid into rings. Heat the oil in a skillet, add the squid and sauté about 4 minutes until cooked through.

5 Drain the pasta and transfer it to a baking dish. To the tomato sauce, add the squid, lemon zest and juice, and the peas and adjust the seasoning if necessary. Pour the sauce into the dish with the pasta and stir well to combine.

6 Beat the egg into the white sauce, then pour the sauce over the pasta mixture. Separate the pasta with a fork in several places so that the white sauce fills the gaps. Level the surface, sprinkle with the bread crumbs, and bake 15 minutes, until golden brown and bubbly. Serve hot.

6

in anticipo

cook ahead

For busy people or those with large families, it is always useful to be able to make tasty fresh pasta sauces, such as traditional Ligurian pesto and its not-so-traditional but equally spirited variations, in advance, when you have the time. Also, when you have just that little bit more time, you can conjure up some of the tasty baked and stuffed pastas, such as lasagne, cannelloni, and ravioli. Many of these are actually all the better for being made ahead, because the flavors then get a chance to mingle and develop.

Mandilli di Seta con Pesto Pasta Squares with Pesto   **serves 2**

In Liguria, where this recipe originated, these are called *mandilli di seta* or "silk handkerchiefs." This pesto is the recipe for Italy's classic basil and pine nut sauce. Make it in the summer, when basil is at its most tender, fragrant, and prolific. You might like to triple the quantity of pesto and store the extra in a jar for future use. Keep it in the refrigerator and always make sure there is enough oil in the jar to cover the pesto, to prevent it from drying out and discoloring.

FOR THE PASTA
1⅓ **cups hard, white unbleached flour, preferably Italian 00-grade (see page 8)**
pinch sea salt
2 extra-large eggs
I tablespoon olive oil

FOR THE PESTO
I **garlic clove, crushed**
2 tablespoons pine nuts
sea salt
2 tablespoons freshly grated Parmesan cheese, plus extra, to serve
I **cup fresh basil leaves**
5 tablespoons fruity extra-virgin olive oil

1 Make the pasta dough as described on page 8 and let it rest in a cool place about 30 minutes.

2 Roll out the pasta dough in a pasta machine as described on page 11. Alternatively, divide the dough into manageable pieces and cover the dough you are not working with. Take each piece of dough and, with the heel of your hand, press it out. Using a long, thin rolling pin and a little flour, gently roll out the dough as thin as you can. Let it dry on a clean dish towel 30 minutes. Cut the pasta into 6-inch squares.

3 To make the pesto, using a mortar and pestle, pound the garlic, pine nuts, and a pinch of salt together. Add the cheese and basil and continue to pound. A little at a time, add the oil, and pound until you have a smooth paste.

4 Cook half of the pasta squares in a large pot of boiling salted water 7 minutes, until al dente, or just tender but still firm to the bite. Drain and toss the pasta with some of the sauce, then serve hot, with cheese. Cook and serve the rest in the same way.

Variations
As these pasta squares are very plain, you can also serve them with other pestos, such as wild arugula pesto, parsley pesto, or mint and lemon pesto (page 112). The walnut sauce for pansotti (page 116) is also extremely good with them.

Tortellini con Ricotta Tortellini with Ricotta   serves 6

Because of their unique shape, tortellini are also known in Italy as "venus navels." Legend has it that Venus and Jupiter had an assignation one night in an inn, and the chef at the inn peeked through the keyhole of Venus's room to see her lying half naked on the bed. The sight of her heavenly navel inspired him to rush to the kitchen and create tortellini in its image.

FOR THE PASTA
4¼ cups hard, white unbleached flour, preferably Italian 00-grade (see page 8)
sea salt
6 extra-large eggs
I tablespoon olive oil
semolina, for sprinkling

FOR THE FILLING
I cup freshly grated Parmesan cheese
⅔ cup ricotta
2 tablespoons truffle condiment (see below)
sea salt and freshly ground black pepper

TO FINISH
knob unsalted butter
fresh basil leaves
freshly grated Parmesan cheese

1 Make the pasta dough as described on page 8 and let it rest in a cool place about 30 minutes.

2 To make the filling, mix together the Parmesan cheese, ricotta, and truffle condiment, with salt and pepper to taste.

3 Roll out the dough in a pasta machine as described on page 11. Alternatively, divide the dough into manageable pieces and cover the dough you are not working with. Take one piece of dough and, with the heel of your hand, press it out. Using a long, thin rolling pin and a little flour, gently roll out the pasta into a paper-thin sheet, sprinkling the surface with semolina. Cut the pasta into 4-inch squares.

4 Place I teaspoonful of filling in the middle of each square. Moisten the edges with water, then fold one corner over to make a triangle, making sure there is little or no trapped air. Press the edges lightly together, bringing the corners of the triangle in toward each other to make a circular shape. Lay the tortellini on baking sheets, sprinkle with semolina, and set aside to dry I hour.

5 Put the tortellini in a large pot of boiling salted water and bring back to a boil. Lower the heat and simmer 4 to 5 minutes, until al dente, or just tender but still firm to the bite. Drain the pasta and serve it, dressed with a little knob of butter and garnished with basil leaves, with extra Parmesan cheese served separately.

Consiglio Sprinkling the pasta with semolina as you roll it out helps the pasta to dry, which makes it easier to handle.

Truffle condiment is a paste of minced truffles, sometimes extended with chopped porcini mushrooms to keep the price down. Available from good Italian delis and some supermarkets, it is expensive, but a little goes a long way.

Variations
Other good stuffings for tortellini include blue cheese, and ham and ricotta.

Pesto di Peperoni Arrostiti con Penne Rigate Roasted Bell Pepper Pesto with Penne Rigate   serves 6

Recently there has been an explosion in variations on classic basil pesto in restaurants, but the Italians themselves have been playing with the concept for generations.

1 pound 2 ounces penne rigate (ridged penne; see page 39)
fresh basil leaves, to garnish

FOR THE PESTO
4 red bell peppers
⅔ cup finely ground blanched almonds
finely chopped zest of 1 unwaxed lemon
4 tablespoons extra-virgin olive oil, plus a little more to finish
1 garlic clove, peeled
2 teaspoons balsamic vinegar
⅓ cup freshly grated Parmesan cheese
sea salt and freshly ground black pepper

1 To make the pesto, heat the oven to 400°F. Put the peppers on a baking sheet and roast them 25 minutes, turning them once; they should become charred and deflated. Let them cool on a wire rack. (This can be done a day ahead.)

2 When the peppers are cool, peel off the skins and remove the seeds; try to save the precious juices from the peppers by holding them over a bowl as you do this.

3 Put the pepper flesh and juices, and all the other pesto ingredients, in the food processor and process until blended, smooth, and thick. Taste and adjust the seasoning with more salt and pepper, if necessary.

4 Cook the pasta in a large pot of boiling salted water until al dente, or just tender but still firm to the bite. Drain the pasta and toss it with the sauce, then garnish with basil leaves and serve.

Consiglio **If you don't want to use the pesto right away, put it in a sterilized jar (it should fill a 1-cup jar) and top it with olive oil, which will act as a preservative. Store it in the refrigerator up to 2 weeks.**

This sauce not only is good with pasta, but also makes an excellent salad dressing, or it can be used to dress steamed fresh vegetables.

Mint and lemon Finely chop a generous handful of fresh mint leaves and mix together the finely grated zest of 2 unwaxed lemons and the juice of 3 lemons. Replace the peppers, almonds, and lemon zest in the basic recipe with this mixture.

Parsley Replace the peppers in the basic recipe with a large bunch of fresh flat-leaf parsley, double the amount of lemon zest, and replace the almonds with pine nuts. This mixture is also good if you use equal parts parsley and cilantro, and both variations are good if you add a seeded chile pepper.

Asparagus Heat the oven to 400°F. Trim a large bunch of asparagus, arrange them on a baking sheet, brush lightly with olive oil, and season with sea salt. Roast 10 minutes, let the asparagus cool, and then coarsely chop it. Use the asparagus in the basic recipe in place of the peppers and replace the almonds with pine nuts.

Wild arugula Wash 2 large bunches of wild arugula well and trim off all the coarse stems. Use the arugula in the basic recipe in place of the peppers and replace the almonds with pine nuts.

Cannelloni con Fave e Ricotta Cannelloni with Fava Beans and Ricotta   serves 6

Here the pasta and/or the sauce can be made ahead, or the whole thing can be assembled and kept for a day or two in the refrigerator before baking—and will actually benefit in terms of flavor.

FOR THE PASTA
I cup flour, preferably Italian 00-grade (see page 8)
I cup semolina, plus more for sprinkling
sea salt
2 extra-large eggs
I tablespoon olive oil

FOR THE FILLING
2¼ pounds fava beans in the pod, podded
1½ cups ricotta
I cup freshly grated Pecorino Romano cheese, plus more to serve
I large garlic clove, crushed
large handful fresh mint, chopped
sea salt and freshly ground black pepper

FOR THE BESCIAMELLA SAUCE
2½ cups milk
2 slices onion
I bay leaf
I blade mace
3 large parsley stems, bruised
5 whole black peppercorns
4 tablespoons butter
⅓ cup all-purpose flour
⅔ cup dry white wine

1 Make the pasta: Heap the flour and semolina into a mound on the work surface. Add a pinch of salt and mix well. Hollow out a well in the center and break in the eggs. Add the oil and, with much care and patience, gradually work the eggs and oil into the flour until you have a slab of dough. Shape it into a ball, cover with a towel or wrap in plastic wrap, and set aside to rest while you prepare the filling.

2 Make the filling: Boil or steam the fava beans until tender, about 10 minutes; drain and let cool. Once cool, put half of the beans in a food processor and pulse, leaving some texture. Add the ricotta, Pecorino Romano, garlic, and mint, with salt and pepper to taste. Add the remaining whole fava beans and mix well with a wooden spoon.

3 Roll out the pasta dough wafer thin and cut into 3-inch squares. Sprinkle lightly with semolina and let dry on a tray 10 to 15 minutes.

4 When almost dry, cook the pasta squares in a large pot of boiling salted water until al dente, or just tender but still firm to the bite. Heat the oven to 400°F.

5 Make the besciamella sauce: Place the milk in a pan with the onion slices, bay leaf, mace, parsley stems, and peppercorns. Heat over medium-low heat and bring to a simmer, then remove from the heat and let infuse 8 to 10 minutes.

6 Melt 2 tablespoons of the butter in a saucepan, stir in the flour, and continue stirring over the heat 1 minute. Remove from the heat, strain in the infused milk, discarding the solids, and stir well. Return to the heat and stir or whisk continuously until boiling. Add the remaining butter and the wine and simmer 3 minutes; season to taste with salt and pepper.

7 On each pasta square, spread 1 tablespoon of the filling and roll it up into a cylinder. Spread half of the besciamella sauce in a baking dish, and arrange the filled cannelloni over the sauce in parallel lines running from the long edge of the dish. Cover with the remaining sauce and sprinkle with the extra Pecorino Romano. Bake 15 minutes. Serve immediately.

Variation
You can use Bolognese sauce (page 134) instead of the besciamella.

Pansotti con Erbe e Formaggi Pansotti with Herbs and Cheese   serves 6 to 8

In Liguria, the dough for their version of ravioli, pansotti, is flavored with white wine, and the stuffing is made of cheese and *preboggion*, a mixture of many different types of fresh local herbs and wild leaves, like beet, borage, dandelion, and wild endive. The dish is traditionally served with a kind of pesto made from walnuts.

½ recipe egg pasta dough (page 8), with a handful of finely chopped parsley and a very small handful finely chopped fresh thyme added to the well

flour for dusting

4 tablespoons unsalted butter

freshly grated Parmesan cheese, to serve

FOR THE FILLING

1 cup plus 2 tablespoons ricotta

1¼ cups freshly grated Parmesan cheese

large handful fresh basil leaves, finely chopped

large handful flat-leaf parsley, finely chopped

few sprigs fresh marjoram or oregano, leaves removed and finely chopped

1 garlic clove, crushed

1 medium egg

sea salt and freshly ground black pepper

FOR THE WALNUT SAUCE

¾ cup shelled fresh walnuts

1 garlic clove

4 tablespoons extra-virgin olive oil

½ cup heavy cream

1 Make the filling: Put the ricotta, Parmesan, chopped basil, parsley, and marjoram, garlic, and egg in a bowl, with salt and pepper to taste; beat well to mix.

2 Make the sauce: Put the walnuts, garlic, and oil, with salt and pepper to taste, in a food processor and process to a paste, adding up to ½ cup warm water to thin the sauce. Spoon the sauce into a large bowl and add the cream. Beat well to mix, then adjust the seasoning, if necessary.

3 Using a pasta machine, roll out one-quarter of the pasta dough into a 30- to 40-inch strip (see page 11). Cut the strip into two 18- to 20-inch pieces. (You can do this during rolling if the strip becomes too long to manage.)

4 Using a 2-inch square ravioli cutter, cut 8 to 10 squares from one of the pasta strips. Mound 1 teaspoon of filling in the middle of each square. Brush a little water around the edge of each square, then fold the square diagonally in half over the filling into a triangular shape, making sure there is little or no trapped air; press the edges gently to seal. Put out the pansotti on clean, floured dish towels, sprinkle lightly with flour, and let dry while you roll, cut and fill the remaining pasta dough to make 64 to 80 pansotti.

5 Put the pansotti in a large pot of boiling salted water, bring back to a boil, lower the heat and poach in gently simmering water 4 to 5 minutes.

6 Meanwhile, put the walnut sauce in a large, warm bowl and add a ladleful of the pasta cooking water to thin it. Melt the butter in a small saucepan until sizzling. Drain the pansotti and transfer them to the bowl of walnut sauce. Drizzle the butter over them. Toss well, then sprinkle with grated Parmesan.

7 Serve immediately, with more grated Parmesan handed around separately.

Consiglio   **Both the pansotti and the walnut sauce can be made a day or two ahead and kept in the refrigerator.**

Culurjones
Sardinian Ravioli   serves 4 to 6

These ravioli, originating in northern Sardinia, can also be served dressed with tomato sauce. The saffron—undoubtedly an inheritance from the days when the Moors and Spanish ruled this island—gives them a very distinctive flavor.

½ recipe egg pasta dough
(see page 8)
flour for dusting
4 tablespoons unsalted butter
½ cup freshly grated Pecorino
Sardo cheese

FOR THE FILLING
2 potatoes, each about
7 ounces, diced
½ cup freshly grated Pecorino
Sardo cheese
3 ounces soft, fresh pecorino
cheese, or soft, fresh goat cheese
1 egg yolk
large bunch fresh mint leaves,
chopped
generous pinch saffron powder
sea salt and freshly ground black
pepper

1 Make the filling: Cook the potatoes in boiling salted water 15 minutes, or until soft. Drain the potatoes and transfer them to a bowl, then mash until smooth; set aside until cold. Add the cheeses, egg yolk, mint, and saffron, with salt and pepper to taste, and stir well to mix.

2 Using a pasta machine, roll out about one-quarter of the pasta dough into a 36- to 40-inch strip. Cut the strip with a sharp knife into two 18- to 20-inch pieces.

3 With a fluted 4-inch round cutter, cut out 4 or 5 circles from one of the pasta strips. Mound 1 heaped teaspoon of filling on one side of each circle. Brush a little water around the edge of each pasta circle, then fold the plain side of the circle over the filling to make a half-moon shape, making sure there is little or no trapped air. Pleat the curved edge to seal.

4 Put the *culurjones* on floured, clean dish towels, sprinkle lightly with flour, and let dry while you roll, cut and fill the remaining pasta dough to make 32 to 40 *culurjones*. If you have any stuffing left, roll the pasta trimmings and make some more *culurjones*.

5 Heat the oven to 375°F. Put the *culurjones* in a large pot of boiling salted water, bring back to a boil, lower the heat and poach in gently simmering water for 4 to 5 minutes. Meanwhile, melt the butter in a small saucepan.

6 Drain the *culurjones*, transfer them to a large baking dish, and pour butter over them. Sprinkle with the grated pecorino and bake 10 to 15 minutes, until golden and bubbling. Let stand 5 minutes, then serve.

Ravioli Fritti Fried Ravioli   serves 6

Pasta is most often boiled or baked, but deep-frying is another excellent method of cooking it. Here the pasta becomes a crisp and delicious wrapper around a hot, melted-cheese filling, flavored with arugula and parsley. The ravioli can be made up to two days in advance and stored in the refrigerator, to be cooked when needed. These make very nice party food, especially if served with a cold tomato sauce as a dip.

FOR THE PASTA
2 cups hard white unbleached flour or all-purpose flour
sea salt
4 tablespoons unsalted butter
I egg, separated, plus I egg yolk
vegetable oil for deep-frying

FOR THE FILLING
4 ounces Gruyère cheese
I cup finely chopped fresh arugula
⅓ cup freshly grated Parmesan cheese
I egg, beaten
handful fresh flat-leaf parsley, finely chopped
sea salt and freshly ground black pepper

1 Make the pasta: Sift the flour and a pinch of salt onto a work surface. Make a well in the middle. Cut the butter into small pieces and add it to the well, along with the egg yolks. Work into a smooth dough, adding a little lukewarm water, if necessary.

2 Make the filling: Grate the Gruyère and put it in a bowl with the arugula, Parmesan, beaten egg, parsley, and salt and pepper to taste; stir well.

3 Flatten the pasta dough with a rolling pin and roll it out into a sheet about ¼ inch thick. Cut into 5-inch circles. Divide the filling among the circles, placing it in the middle of each one. Lightly whisk the egg white. Brush the edge of each circle with a little egg white, then fold the pasta over the filling to enclose it completely, making sure there is little or no trapped air, and pinch to seal the edge.

4 Heat the oil to 375°F. Drop in the ravioli, a few at a time, and fry until golden brown. Drain on paper towels while frying the remaining ravioli. Serve hot.

Variation
These ravioli are also delicious stuffed with Bolognese Sauce (page 134).

Tortellini con Burro e Salvia Tortellini with Butter and Sage   serves 6

This Umbrian dish is one of those that I cook regularly, because it never disappoints. Sage is yet another ingredient valued by the Italians; it is said to clarify the mind.

FOR THE PASTA
1 ½ cups hard white unbleached flour, preferably Italian 00-grade (see page 8), plus extra for dusting
sea salt
2 extra-large eggs
I tablespoon olive oil

FOR THE FILLING
½ cup ricotta
2 ounces Fontina cheese
½ cup freshly grated Parmesan cheese
I egg, beaten
pinch freshly grated nutmeg
handful fresh sage leaves, finely chopped

TO FINISH
4 tablespoons unsalted butter
handful fresh sage leaves
freshly grated Parmesan cheese

1 Make the pasta dough as described on page 8 and let rest in a cool place 30 minutes.

2 Mix together all the filling ingredients and beat thoroughly.

3 Roll out the dough in a pasta machine as described on page 11. Alternatively, divide the dough into manageable pieces and cover those you are not working with. Take one piece of dough and, with the heel of your hand, press it out. Using a long, thin rolling pin and a little flour, roll out the dough to a paper-thin sheet. Cut the pasta into 2-inch circles. Place small spoonfuls of the filling on one side of each circle, dampen the edge, then fold the dough over the filling to make a half-moon shape (don't worry, the two edges won't quite meet), making sure there is little or no trapped air; press down to seal the edge. Curl the rounded triangle around one of your index fingers, bringing the 2 corners together, and press these together to seal. Let dry briefly on a flour-dusted tray.

4 Put the tortellini in a large pot of boiling salted water, adding a handful at a time, bring back to a boil, lower the heat and poach in gently simmering water 3 to 5 minutes. When they rise to the top of the pan, count 30 seconds, then remove them with a slotted spoon and place them in a warm serving dish.

5 Melt the butter and pour it over the tortellini. Garnish with sage leaves and serve with a sprinkling of Parmesan.

Consiglio **The tortellini can be prepared in advance and kept in the refrigerator up to 2 days.**

Variation
Try frying the sage leaves in olive oil until crisp before scattering them over the tortellini.

Pappardelle con Sugo di Coniglio
Pappardelle with Rabbit Sauce   serves 4

This is a slightly tamer version of the ancient Tuscan classic dish, *pappardelle con lepre* (with hare sauce), generally held to be among the most delicious of all pasta dishes.

1 ounce dried porcini mushrooms

1 onion

1 carrot

1 celery rib

3 bay leaves

2 tablespoons unsalted butter

1 tablespoon olive oil

2 ounces pancetta, diced

handful fresh flat-leaf parsley, roughly chopped, plus extra to serve

9 ounces boneless rabbit meat

6 tablespoons dry white wine

half 14½-ounce can crushed Italian plum tomatoes

sea salt and freshly ground black pepper

7 ounces dried pappardelle (see page 58)

1 Put the porcini in a bowl, pour ½ cup warm water over, and let soak 10 to 15 minutes. Finely chop the onion, carrot and celery, either in a food processor or by hand. Make a tear in each of the bay leaves to help release their flavor.

2 Heat the butter and oil in a medium-size saucepan until just sizzling. Add the vegetables, pancetta, and parsley and fry 5 minutes.

3 Add the rabbit meat and fry on all sides 3 to 4 minutes. Pour in the wine and let it reduce for a few minutes, then add the tomatoes. Drain the porcini and pour the soaking liquid into the pan. Chop the mushrooms and add them to the mixture, along with the bay leaves and salt and pepper to taste. Stir well, cover, and simmer 35 to 45 minutes, until the rabbit is tender, stirring occasionally.

4 Remove the pan from the heat and lift out the rabbit pieces with a draining spoon. Cut them into bite-size chunks and stir them back into the sauce. Remove and discard the bay leaves. Taste and adjust the seasoning, if necessary.

5 Cook the pasta in a large pot of boiling salted water until al dente, or just tender but still firm to the bite.

6 Reheat the sauce, if necessary. Drain the pasta and toss it with the sauce in a warm bowl. Serve immediately, sprinkled with parsley.

Consiglio This sauce is one that definitely improves in flavor for being made at least a day ahead and then reheated.

Spaghetti con Polpettini di Vitello Spaghetti with Veal Meatballs serves 6 to 8

This is a classic southern dish that has become a standard in American home cooking.

12 ounces dried spaghetti

freshly grated Parmesan cheese, to serve

FOR THE MEATBALLS AND SAUCE
12 ounces ground veal
I egg
2 tablespoons roughly chopped fresh flat-leaf parsley, plus extra to serve
sea salt and freshly ground black pepper
I thick slice white bread, crusts removed
2 tablespoons milk
3 tablespoons olive oil
1¼ cups tomato puree
1¾ cups vegetable stock (page 19)
I teaspoon sugar

1 Make the meatballs: Put the veal in a large bowl. Add the egg and half of the parsley and season with salt and pepper. Tear the bread into small pieces and place it in a small bowl. Moisten with the milk and let it soak for a few minutes. Squeeze out the excess milk and crumble the bread over the meat mixture. Mix everything together with a wooden spoon, then use your hands to squeeze and knead the mixture so it becomes smooth and sticky.

2 Wash your hands, rinse them under cold water, then pick up small pieces of the mixture and roll them between the palms of your hands to make 40 to 60 small balls. Place the meatballs on a tray and chill in the refrigerator 30 minutes.

3 Heat the oil in a large skillet and fry the meatballs in batches until brown on all sides.

4 Pour the tomato puree and stock into a large saucepan and heat slowly. Add the sugar, with salt and pepper to taste. Add the meatballs, then bring to a boil. Lower the heat, cover, and simmer 20 minutes.

5 Cook the pasta in a large pot of boiling salted water until al dente, or just tender but still firm to the bite.

6 Drain the pasta and transfer it to a large warm bowl. Pour the sauce over the pasta and toss gently. Sprinkle with the remaining parsley and serve with Parmesan cheese.

Ravioli alla Romagnola Ravioli with Pork and Turkey   serves 6 to 8

This Roman-style ravioli, stuffed with ground meat and cheese and scented with fresh herbs, makes an absolutely delicious dish.

½ recipe egg pasta dough (see page 8)
flour for dusting
2 ounces butter
large bunch of fresh sage, leaves removed and roughly chopped, plus more to serve
4 tablespoons freshly grated Parmesan cheese, plus extra to serve

FOR THE FILLING
2 tablespoons butter
5 ounces ground pork
4 ounces ground turkey
4 fresh sage leaves, finely chopped
1 rosemary sprig, leaves removed and finely chopped
sea salt and freshly ground black pepper
2 tablespoons dry white wine
⅓ cup ricotta
3 tablespoons grated Parmesan cheese
1 egg
freshly grated nutmeg

1 Make the filling: Melt the butter in a medium-size saucepan. Add the pork, turkey, and the herbs and cook slowly 5 to 6 minutes, stirring frequently and breaking up the meat with a wooden spoon. Add salt and pepper to taste and stir well to mix thoroughly.

2 Add the wine to the pan and stir again. Simmer 1 to 2 minutes, until reduced slightly, then cover the pan and simmer slowly 20 minutes, stirring occasionally. Using a slotted spoon, transfer the meat to a bowl and let cool completely.

3 Add the ricotta and Parmesan to the meat, together with the egg and add nutmeg to taste. Stir well to mix the ingredients thoroughly.

4 Using a pasta machine, roll out one-quarter of the pasta dough into a 36- to 40-inch strip. Cut the strip with a sharp knife into two 18- to 20-inch pieces. (You can do this during rolling if the strips become too long to manage.)

5 Using a teaspoon, put 10 to 12 little mounds of the filling along one side of one of the pasta strips, spacing them evenly. Brush a little water onto the pasta strip around each mound, then fold the plain side of the pasta strip over the filling. Starting from the folded edge, press down gently with your fingertip around each mound of filling, pushing the air out at the unfolded edge; sprinkle lightly with flour.

6 With a fluted pasta wheel, cut along each long side in between each mound to make small square shapes; dust lightly with flour. Put the ravioli in a single layer on floured clean dish towels and let dry while filling and cutting the remaining pasta dough to make 80 to 96 ravioli.

7 Drop the ravioli into a large pot of boiling salted water, bring back to a boil, lower the heat and poach in gently simmering water 4 to 5 minutes. Meanwhile, melt the butter in a small pan.

8 Remove the ravioli with a slotted spoon as they are cooked and serve dressed with the melted butter, sage and Parmesan.

Lasagne alla Bolognese Lasagne Bolognese   serves 6

This is the classic lasagne, based on a rich, meaty filling, as you would expect from an authentic bolognese recipe.

1 recipe **Bolognese sauce**
(page 134)

1 recipe besciamella sauce
(page 129)

²⁄₃ **to 1 cup hot beef stock**

12 no-need-to-precook dried
lasagne sheets

¹⁄₂ **cup freshly grated Parmesan**
cheese

1 Heat the oven to 375°F. If the sauces are cold, reheat them gently . Once it is hot, stir just enough of the stock into the Bolognese sauce to make it runny.

2 Spread about one-third of the Bolognese sauce over the bottom of a 9-x-11-inch baking dish. Cover this with about one-quarter of the besciamella sauce, followed by 4 sheets lasagne. Repeat the layers twice more, then cover the top layer of lasagne with the remaining besciamella sauce. Sprinkle the cheese evenly over the top.

3 Bake 40 minutes, until the pasta feels tender when pierced with a skewer. Let stand 10 minutes, then serve.

Consiglio **The Bolognese sauce can be made up to 3 days in advance and kept in a covered container in the refrigerator.**

To reheat leftover lasagne, prick it all over with a skewer, then slowly pour a little milk on top to moisten. Cover with foil and place in the oven heated to 375°F ; bake 20 minutes, or until bubbling.

Do not reheat lasagne if the meat sauce was made in advance, because it can be dangerous to reheat meat dishes more than once.

Variations
Make a meatless version using a spicy tomato sauce (page 105, adding some crushed dried chile flakes to taste) instead of the Bolognese. Alternatively, omit the Bolognese sauce and layer in some fresh spinach and sun-dried tomatoes.

Consiglio **Using Italian 00-grade flour produces a lighter white sauce.**

Lasagne con Polpettini Lasagne with Meatballs serves 6 to 8

11 ounces ground beef
11 ounces ground pork
1 extra-large egg
1 cup fresh white bread crumbs
5 tablespoons freshly grated
Parmesan cheese
2 tablespoons chopped fresh
flat-leaf parsley, plus extra
to garnish
2 garlic cloves, crushed
sea salt and freshly ground black
pepper
4 tablespoons olive oil
1 onion, finely chopped
1 carrot, finely chopped
1 celery rib, finely chopped
two 14½-ounce cans crushed
Italian plum tomatoes
2 teaspoons finely chopped fresh
oregano or basil
6 to 8 no-need-to-precook dried
lasagne sheets

FOR THE BESCIAMELLA SAUCE
3 cups milk
1 bay leaf
1 fresh thyme sprig
4 tablespoons unsalted butter
⅓ cup Italian 00-grade flour or
all-purpose flour
freshly grated nutmeg

1 First make the meatballs: Put 6 ounces each of the beef and pork in a large bowl. Add the egg, bread crumbs, 2 tablespoons of the cheese, half of the parsley, half of the garlic, and plenty of salt and pepper. Mix everything together with a wooden spoon, then use your hands to squeeze and knead the mixture so it becomes smooth and sticky.

2 Wash your hands and rinse them under cold water, then pick up small pieces of the mixture and roll them between your palms to make about 30 walnut-size balls. Place on a tray and chill in the refrigerator 30 minutes.

3 Meanwhile, put the milk for the besciamella sauce in a saucepan. Make a tear in the bay leaf, then add it and the thyme sprig to the milk and bring to a boil. Remove from the heat, cover, and set aside to infuse.

4 Make the meat sauce: Heat half of the oil in a medium-size pan. Add the onion, carrot, celery, and the remaining garlic and stir over low heat 5 minutes, or until soft. Add the remaining meat and cook slowly 10 minutes, stirring frequently and breaking up any lumps. Stir in salt and pepper to taste, then add the tomatoes, the remaining parsley, and the oregano. Stir well, cover, and simmer 45 to 60 minutes, stirring occasionally.

5 Meanwhile, heat the remaining oil in a large nonstick skillet over medium to high heat. When hot, cook the meatballs in batches 5 to 8 minutes, until brown all over. Shake the pan from time to time so the meatballs roll around. As they cook, transfer them to paper towels to drain.

6 Heat the oven to 375°F. Finish the besciamella sauce: Strain the milk and discard the bay leaf and thyme. Melt the butter in a medium-size pan. Add the flour and cook, stirring, 1 to 2 minutes. Add the infused milk, a little at a time, whisking vigorously after each addition. Bring to a boil and cook, stirring constantly, until thick and smooth. Grate in a little nutmeg to taste and season with salt and pepper. Whisk well, then remove from the heat.

7 Spread about one-third of the meat sauce in the bottom of a large, shallow baking dish. Add half of the meatballs, then spread with one-third of the besciamella and cover with half the lasagne sheets. Repeat these layers, then top with the remaining meat sauce and besciamella. Sprinkle the remaining cheese evenly over the surface.

8 Bake 30 to 40 minutes until golden brown and bubbling. Let stand 10 minutes, then serve. If you like, garnish each serving with parsley.

impressionante
pasta to impress

Pasta has become so much a part of everyday family eating in most countries outside Italy that people often look askance at me when I suggest serving it at dinner parties or for special occasions. Nevertheless, pasta can be rich and luxurious, and every bit as impressive as roast meat or an elaborate layered chef's extravaganza. Certain ingredients immediately endow pasta with that touch of class—crab and lobster in fillings for stuffed pasta, say, or saffron to color the pasta. Some techniques do it, like open layered lasagne (*vincisgrassi aperto*) or stuffed rolls of pasta, sliced and broiled (*rotolo ripieno*). Essentially, however, the dishes remain simple, and it is the shape of the pasta and dramatic or unusual presentation that do the job.

Agnolotti con Taleggio e Maggiorana Agnolotti with Taleggio and Marjoram
serves 6 as an appetizer, 4 as a main course

The filling for these little half moons is simple, but the combination is very effective.

½ recipe fresh egg pasta dough (see page 8)

12 ounces Taleggio cheese

about 2 tablespoons finely chopped fresh marjoram, plus extra to garnish

sea salt and freshly ground black pepper

flour for dusting

½ cup (1 stick) unsalted butter

freshly grated Parmesan cheese, to serve

1 Using a pasta machine, roll out one-quarter of the pasta dough into a 36- to 40-inch strip. Cut the strip with a sharp knife into two 18- to 20-inch pieces.

2 Cut 8 to 10 little cubes of Taleggio and place them along one side of one of the pasta strips, spacing them evenly. Sprinkle each Taleggio cube with a little chopped marjoram, and pepper to taste. Brush a little water around each cube of cheese, then fold the plain side of the pasta strip over them. Starting from the folded edge, press down gently with your fingertip around each cube, pushing the air out at the unfolded edge; sprinkle lightly with flour.

3 Using only half of a 2-inch fluted round cookie cutter, cut the pasta around each cube of cheese to make half-moon shapes: The folded edge should be the straight edge. If you like, press the cut edges of the agnolotti with the tines of a fork to give a decorative effect. Put the agnolotti on floured, clean dish towels, sprinkle lightly with flour, and let dry while you fill and cut the remaining pasta dough to make 64 to 80 agnolotti.

4 Drop the agnolotti into a large pot of boiling salted water, bring back to a boil, lower the heat and poach in gently simmering water 4 to 5 minutes, until al dente, or just tender but still firm to the bite.

5 Meanwhile, melt the butter in a small saucepan. Drain the agnolotti and divide them equally among 6 or 8 large warm serving bowls. Drizzle the sizzling butter over them and serve immediately, sprinkled with Parmesan and more marjoram. Hand around more grated Parmesan cheese separately.

Consiglio **Marjoram is traditional with the Taleggio cheese in this recipe, both for the filling and the sizzling butter, but you can use other fresh herbs, such as sage, basil, or flat-leaf parsley.**

Tagliarini al Tartufo Bianco Tagliarini with White Truffle   serves 4

There is nothing quite like the fragrance and flavor of the white truffle. It is one of the rarest and there-fore most expensive of truffles, and comes from around the town of Alba, in Piedmont. This simple style of serving it is one of the best ways to enjoy it. Tagliarini, or tagliolini, is like a thinner tagliatelle.

12 ounces fresh or dried tagliarini (see above)

sea salt and freshly ground black pepper

6 tablespoons unsalted butter, diced

4 tablespoons freshly grated Parmesan cheese

1 teaspoon freshly grated nutmeg

1 small white truffle (about 1 ounce)

1 Cook the pasta in a large pot of boiling salted water until al dente, or just tender but still firm to the bite.

2 Drain the pasta thoroughly and transfer it to a large, warm bowl. Add the butter, cheese, nutmeg, and a little salt and pepper to taste. Toss until the pasta is well coated.

3 Divide the pasta equally among 4 warm bowls and shave paper-thin slivers of the white truffle on top. Serve immediately.

Consiglio   White truffles can be bought during the months of September and October.

Pappardelle con Tartufi e Porcini Pappardelle with Truffles and Porcini   serves 2

2 ounces dried sliced porcini mushrooms

7 ounces dried pappardelle (long, broad pasta; see page 58)

sea salt and freshly ground black pepper

1 tablespoon olive oil

1 garlic clove, crushed

4 tablespoons truffle condiment (see page 109)

2 tablespoons mascarpone cheese

1 tablespoons dry white wine

Parmesan cheese shavings, to serve

1 Soak the dried porcini in cold water to cover 20 minutes, then drain. (Strain the soaking water into the pasta water or use it to thin the sauce, if you like.)

2 Cook the pasta in a large pot of boiling salted water about 12 minutes, until al dente, or just tender but still firm to the bite.

3 Meanwhile, heat the oil in a pan. Add the garlic, truffle condiment, and porcini and cook slowly 10 minutes. Stir in the mascarpone cheese and wine, with salt and pepper to taste.

4 Drain the pasta and toss it in the truffle and porcini mixture. Serve scattered with the Parmesan shavings.

Cappellacci alla Bolognese Cheese Cappellacci with Bolognese Sauce

serves 6 to 8 generously

In Emilia-Romagna it is traditional to serve these cappellacci with a rich meat sauce, but, if you prefer, you can serve them with a tomato sauce or just melted butter.

½ recipe fresh egg pasta dough (page 8)

flour, for dusting

2½ quarts beef stock (page 31)

freshly grated Parmesan cheese, to serve

fresh basil leaves, to garnish

FOR THE FILLING

1 cup plus 2 tablespoons ricotta

3 ounces Taleggio cheese, rind removed, diced very small

4 tablespoons freshly grated Parmesan cheese

1 medium egg

freshly grated nutmeg

sea salt and freshly ground black pepper

FOR THE BOLOGNESE SAUCE

2 tablespoons butter

1 tablespoon olive oil

1 onion, finely chopped

2 carrots, finely chopped

2 celery ribs, finely chopped

2 garlic cloves, finely chopped

1 cup pancetta cut into small cubes

9 ounces lean ground pork

9 ounces lean ground beef

½ cup dry white wine

two 14½-ounce cans crushed Italian plum tomatoes

2 to 3 cups beef stock (page 31)

7 tablespoons heavy cream

1 Make the filling: Put the ricotta, Taleggio, and Parmesan in a bowl and mash together with a fork. Add the egg, a pinch of freshly grated nutmeg, and salt and pepper to taste and stir well to mix.

2 Using a pasta machine, roll out one-quarter of the pasta dough into a 36- to 40-inch strip. Cut the strip with a sharp knife into two 18- to 20-inch pieces. Using a 2½- to 3-inch square ravioli cutter, cut 6 or 7 squares from one of the pasta strips. Mound 1 teaspoon of filling in the middle of each square. Brush a little water around the edge of each square, then fold the square diagonally in half over the filling to make a triangle; press to seal the edges. Wrap the triangle around one of your index fingers, bringing 2 corners together. Pinch the ends together to seal, then press with your fingertips around the top edge of the filling to make an indentation so the "hat" looks like a bishop's miter. Put the cappellacci on floured, clean dish towels, sprinkle with flour, and let dry while you cut and fill the remaining pasta dough to make 48 to 56 cappellacci.

3 Make the Bolognese sauce: Heat the butter and oil in a large saucepan until sizzling. Add the vegetables, garlic, and pancetta and fry over medium heat, stirring frequently, 10 minutes, or until the vegetables are soft. Add the meats, lower the heat, and cook slowly 10 minutes, stirring frequently and breaking up the meat with a wooden spoon. Stir in salt and pepper to taste, then add the wine and stir again. Simmer, uncovered, about 5 minutes, until reduced.

4 Add the tomatoes and 1 cup of the stock and bring to a boil. Stir well, then lower the heat, half cover the pan, and simmer very slowly 2 hours. Stir occasionally during this time and add more stock as it becomes absorbed.

5 Add the cream to the meat sauce. Stir well to mix, then simmer the sauce 30 minutes longer, stirring frequently.

6 Bring the 2½ quarts stock to a boil in a large pot over high heat. Drop the cappellacci into it, bring it back to a boil, lower the heat and poach in gently simmering stock 4 to 5 minutes. Drain the cappellacci and divide them among 6 to 8 warmed bowls. Spoon the hot Bolognese sauce over the cappellacci and sprinkle with the Parmesan and basil leaves. Serve immediately.

Rotolo Ripieno Spinach, Ricotta, and Tomato Pasta Roll   serves 4

I first enjoyed this pasta dish while on vacation in Umbria. I was so impressed with the unique way of broiling the pasta to give it a crunchy outer texture and the stylish presentation that I begged for the recipe. Eventually, after patronizing the restaurant on five consecutive days, the chef relented to my entreaties, so here is the recipe for you to enjoy too.

$^1/_2$ recipe egg pasta dough (page 8)

2 tablespoons unsalted butter, melted, plus more for greasing and serving

$^1/_2$ cup freshly grated Parmesan cheese

FOR THE FILLING

4 plum tomatoes

12 ounces fresh spinach

$^3/_4$ cup ricotta

freshly grated nutmeg

sea salt and freshly ground black pepper

$^1/_2$ cup freshly grated Parmesan cheese

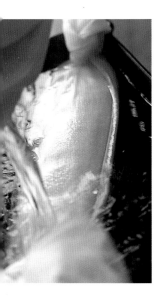

1 Start preparing the filling: Put the tomatoes in a bowl, cover with boiling water for about 40 seconds, then plunge them into cold water; peel them and chop the flesh.

2 Put the spinach in a saucepan with only the water still clinging to the leaves after washing them. Cook about 5 minutes over medium-high heat, then drain the spinach well, squeezing out as much excess water from the leaves as you can.

3 Finely chop the spinach and put it in a bowl. Add the tomatoes and ricotta, with nutmeg, salt, and pepper to taste, and mix together with the Parmesan.

4 Roll the pasta dough out into a rectangular sheet about $^1/_8$ inch thick. Place it on a large piece of cheesecloth and spread the filling over the dough, leaving a 1$^1/_4$-inch border clear around the edge. Lifting one end of the cheesecloth, roll up the dough like a jelly roll. Wrap it in the cheesecloth and secure the ends with string.

5 Place the roll in a long, narrow flameproof casserole, roasting pan, or fish poacher and cover with lightly salted cold water. Bring to a boil and simmer 30 minutes. Remove from the water and let cool 5 minutes. Meanwhile, heat the broiler.

6 Remove the cheesecloth and cut the roll into slices about $^3/_4$ inch thick. Place these side by side, or slightly overlapping, in a buttered baking dish. Pour the butter over the slices and sprinkle them with the Parmesan.

7 Broil 5 minutes, until golden. Serve immediately, straight from the dish or on individual plates, sprinkled with a little black pepper and more melted butter or extra-virgin olive oil.

Consiglio   The pasta roll can be made in advance and kept in the refrigerator up to 2 days. First, let it return to room temperature, then slice and broil as above. Also, leftover pasta can be used like pastry, to line, say, a pie or quiche dish.

Garganelli con Asparagi e Panna Garganelli with Asparagus and Cream serves 4

A specialty of Romagna, garganelli are made from little squares of pasta rolled into quill shapes and then grooved.

9 to 12 ounces fresh young asparagus
sea salt and freshly ground black pepper
12 ounces dried garganelli (see above)
2 tablespoons unsalted butter
1 cup heavy cream
2 tablespoons dry white wine
¾ to 1 cup freshly grated Parmesan cheese
2 tablespoons chopped mixed fresh herbs, such as basil, flat-leaf parsley, marjoram, and oregano

1 Trim off and throw away the woody ends of the asparagus. (After trimming you should have about 7 ounces of asparagus spears.) Cut the spears at an angle into pieces that are roughly the same length and shape as the garganelli.

2 Reserving the tips, blanch the asparagus spears in boiling salted water 2 minutes, adding the tips for the second minute only. Immediately drain the asparagus and rinse in cold water; set aside.

3 Cook the pasta in a large pot of boiling salted water until al dente, or just tender but still firm to the bite.

4 Meanwhile, put the butter and cream in a medium-size saucepan over high heat. Add salt and pepper to taste and bring to a boil. Reduce the heat and simmer a few minutes, until the cream reduces slightly and thickens. Add the asparagus, wine, and about half the Parmesan. Taste and adjust the seasoning, if necessary. Keep over a low heat.

5 Drain the pasta and transfer it to a warm bowl. Pour the sauce over, sprinkle with the herbs, and toss well. Serve topped with the remaining Parmesan.

Tagliatelle con Radicchio e Panna Tagliatelle with Radicchio and Cream serves 4

I recommend long and thin radicchio di Treviso for this recipe, but radicchio rotondo works just as well.

8 ounces dried tagliatelle
salt and freshly ground black pepper
½ cup diced pancetta or slab bacon
2 tablespoons unsalted butter
1 onion, finely chopped
2 to 2½ cups shredded radicchio
1 garlic clove, finely chopped
⅔ cup heavy cream
½ cup freshly grated Parmesan cheese
handful fresh flat-leaf parsley, chopped

1 Cook the pasta in a large pot of boiling salted water until al dente, or just tender but still firm to the bite.

2 Meanwhile, gently heat the pancetta in a pan until the fat runs. Raise the heat and sauté 5 minutes. Add the butter, onion, and radicchio and sauté 4 minutes. Add the garlic and sauté 1 minute longer until the onion is lightly colored. Pour in the cream and add the Parmesan, seasoning to taste with salt and pepper. Stir 1 to 2 minutes, until bubbling; adjust the seasoning.

3 Drain the pasta, transfer it to a bowl, pour the sauce over, and toss together with the parsley.

Cannelloni allo Zafferano Cannelloni with Saffron Sauce   serves 2

This northern dish is perfect for entertaining, because it can be made ahead of time. The delicious cheesy artichoke filling and the elegant mascarpone and saffron sauce never fail to impress.

4 sheets lasagne, each about 6½ x 5 inches
sea salt and freshly ground black pepper

FOR THE FILLING
2 tablespoons olive oil
1 small onion, chopped
4 canned artichoke hearts, drained, rinsed, and chopped
⅓ cup chopped mozzarella cheese
½ cup ricotta cheese
2 ounces Dolcelatte cheese
1 teaspoon finely chopped fresh rosemary

FOR THE SAUCE
1 tablespoon unsalted butter
½ garlic clove, crushed
large pinch saffron threads
1 tablespoon white wine
½ cup mascarpone cheese
sea salt and freshly ground black pepper

1 Heat the oven to 350°F. Put the pasta in a large pot of boiling salted water and bring back to a boil. Boil 1 to 2 minutes, then drain and rinse under cold water.

2 Make the filling: Heat the oil in a saucepan over medium heat. Add the onion and fry until soft. Add the artichoke hearts and sauté 5 minutes. Add the mozzarella, ricotta, Dolcelatte, and rosemary. Season well with salt and pepper and mix well.

3 Make the sauce: Melt the butter in a saucepan. Add the garlic and saffron and heat slowly. Add the wine and mascarpone, with salt and pepper to taste, and simmer 5 minutes.

4 To assemble the dish, place some filling along the middle of each pasta sheet. Moisten the edges with water and roll up each rectangle from one of its narrow edges to form a thick tube. Arrange the cannelloni in a greased baking dish, pour the sauce over, and cover the dish with foil.

5 Bake 20 minutes; serve immediately.

Consiglio **For best results, prepare the sauce the day before you are going to serve it, to allow the flavors to mature.**

Variation
The saffron sauce will also give a touch of elegance to cappellacci stuffed with a Bolognese sauce (page 134) or cannelloni with a fava bean filling (page 114).

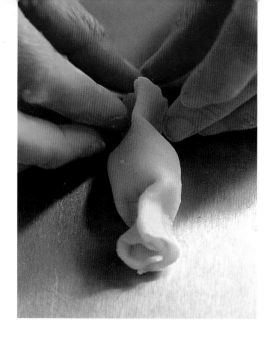

Bonbons con Funghi di Bosco e Ricotta Rolls Filled with Wild Mushrooms and Ricotta

serves 6 as an appetizer, 4 as a main course

These bonbons are best made with thinly rolled homemade pasta, as per the recipe on page 8, but using only 7 ounces of each flour and 4 eggs.

6 sheets of egg pasta dough (see above), about 11 x 9½ inches
I egg, lightly beaten
sea salt
light cream or melted butter
freshly grated Parmesan cheese

FOR THE FILLING
3 cups finely chopped wild mushrooms
2 cups finely chopped portobello mushrooms
½ onion, grated
⅔ cup ricotta
2 tablespoons freshly grated Parmesan cheese
½ teaspoon finely chopped fresh sage
½ teaspoon finely chopped fresh oregano
½ teaspoon finely chopped fresh flat-leaf parsley leaves
pinch freshly grated nutmeg
freshly ground black pepper

1 Cut each pasta sheet into 9 rectangles, each about 3 x 2 inches. Using a scalloped pastry wheel, trim the shorter ends of each rectangle.

2 Mix all the filling ingredients together. Place 1 teaspoon filling in the middle of each pasta rectangle. Brush the beaten egg along one long side and fold the pasta to form a tube. Press to seal, trying to remove as much trapped air as possible, then pinch and twist the ends tightly, like a candy wrapper. As each roll is shaped, set it aside, uncovered, to rest.

3 Drop the rolls, a few at a time, into a large pot of boiling salted water, bring back to a boil, lower the heat and poach in gently simmering water 4 to 5 minutes, until just tender. Remove with a slotted spoon and pile into a warm serving dish.

4 Toss in the cream and sprinkle with Parmesan; serve immediately.

Variation
These stuffed pastas also suit an herb or spinach and ricotta filling (see pages 116 and 137).

Ravioli al Granchio Ravioli with Crab   serves 4

I first enjoyed this ravioli with crab in Venice—indisputably the home of the finest crab in Italy. It makes a super dinner-party dish and is relatively straightforward.

½ recipe egg pasta dough
(page 8)
flour for dusting
6 tablespoons unsalted butter
juice of 1 lemon

FOR THE FILLING
¾ cup mascarpone cheese
6 ounces crabmeat
handful finely chopped
fresh flat-leaf parsley
finely grated zest of 1 unwaxed
lemon
sea salt and freshly ground black
pepper

1 Make the filling: Put the mascarpone in a bowl, mash well with a fork, and add the crabmeat, parsley, and lemon zest, with salt and pepper to taste; stir well.

2 Using a pasta machine, roll out one-quarter of the pasta into a 36- to 40-inch strip. Using a sharp knife, cut the strip into four 18- to 20-inch pieces (You can do this during the rolling if the strip gets too long to manage.) Using a 2½-inch fluted cookie cutter, cut out 8 circles from each pasta strip.

3 Mound 1 teaspoon of filling in the middle of half of the circles of pasta dough. Brush a little water around the edge of a filled circle, then top each with another circle and press the edges to seal, trying to eliminate as much trapped air as you can. For a decorative finish, press the edges with the tines of a fork. Put the ravioli on a floured dish, sprinkle lightly with flour, and let dry while you cut and fill the remaining pasta dough circles to make 32 ravioli.

4 Add the ravioli to a large pot of boiling salted water, bring back to a boil, lower the heat and poach in gently simmering water 4 to 5 minutes.

5 Meanwhile, melt the butter together with the lemon juice until sizzling. Drain the ravioli and divide them equally among 4 warm bowls. Drizzle the lemon butter over the ravioli and serve immediately.

Consiglio **You can use all white crabmeat or a mixture of white and dark. If you use dark meat, the flavor will obviously be much stronger.**

lobster and herbs
Bring a large pot of heavily salted water with 2 fresh bay leaves in it to a rapid boil and drop in a whole live lobster. Boil 20 minutes, then remove from the water and let cool. Crack open the lobster and its claws and remove all the meat. Use this instead of the crabmeat. If there is more than you need, use the leftover in a salad.

spinach and ricotta
In a tightly closed pot, cook 1 pound young spinach leaves in just the water that clings to their leaves after washing for a few minutes, then squeeze out as much water as possible from them. (Try pressing the spinach between 2 matching plates.) Roughly chop and mix in ½ cup ricotta, some salt and pepper, and perhaps a little lemon juice and some freshly grated nutmeg.

walnut, ricotta, and basil
Chop 1½ cups shelled walnuts and a good handful of fresh basil leaves. Mix well with ½ cup ricotta, the finely grated zest of 1 unwaxed lemon, 2 finely chopped garlic cloves, and salt and pepper to taste.

pumpkin, sage, and ricotta
Cook 3 cups peeled and chopped pumpkin until tender, then mash together with ½ cup ricotta; mix in a handful chopped fresh sage leaves, ¾ cup grated Parmesan cheese, and plenty of salt and pepper.

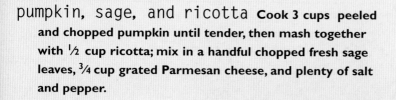

Tagliatelle con Capesanti Tagliatelle with Scallops   serves 4

7 ounces scallops, sliced horizontally into circles
2 tablespoons all-purpose flour
sea salt and freshly ground black pepper
3 tablespoons unsalted butter
1 small onion, finely chopped
1 small fresh red chile, seeded and minced
2 tablespoons finely chopped fresh flat-leaf parsley
4 tablespoons brandy
7 tablespoons fish stock
12 ounces tagliatelle

1 Toss the scallops in the flour; shake off the excess. Bring a large pot of salted water to a boil.

2 Meanwhile, melt the butter in a saucepan over medium heat. Add the onion, chile, and half the parsley and fry, stirring frequently, 1 to 2 minutes. Add the scallops and toss over the heat 1 to 2 minutes.

3 Pour the brandy over the scallops and immediately (and carefully) set it alight with a match. As soon as the flames die down, stir in the fish stock, and salt and pepper to taste; mix well. Simmer 2 to 3 minutes, then cover the pan and remove it from the heat.

4 Add the pasta to the boiling water and cook it until al dente, or just tender but still firm to the bite.

5 Drain the pasta, add it to the sauce, and toss over medium heat until combined. Serve at once, sprinkled with the remaining parsley.

Consiglio **Buy fresh scallops with their coral, if possible. They always have a better texture and flavor than frozen scallops, which will always be very watery. Divers' scallops are better than the more common dredged ones—you can usually tell the latter because their shells are more likely to be scraped and damaged.**

Chiaroscuro Squid Ink Pasta with Ricotta and Scallops serves 4

Versions of this very dramatic-looking dish are served in fashionable restaurants in Italy. I have added tiny queen scallops to make it even more of a special-occasion treat. Obviously, the Italian name comes from the word for the treatment of light and shade in a painting.

12 ounces fresh or dried spaghetti nero (squid ink pasta; pages 8 to 12)
sea salt and freshly ground black pepper
4 tablespoons ricotta (as fresh as possible)
4 tablespoons extra-virgin olive oil
about 20 queen scallops
1 small fresh red chile, seeded and finely chopped
small handful fresh basil leaves

1 Cook the pasta in a large pot of boiling salted water until al dente, or just tender but still firm to the bite.

2 Meanwhile, put the ricotta in a bowl, add salt and pepper to taste, and use a little of the hot water from the pasta pot to mix it to a smooth, creamy consistency. Taste and adjust the seasoning again.

3 Heat a little of the oil in a large skillet over high heat. When it is very hot, add the scallops and sear for no more than 1 minute on each side. Season with salt and pepper, remove from the heat, and keep warm.

4 Drain the pasta and rinse out the pan. Heat the rest of the oil gently in the clean pan and add the pasta along with the chile and salt and pepper to taste. Toss quickly over high heat to combine.

5 Divide the pasta equally among 4 warm bowls, then top with the ricotta mixture. Sprinkle with the cooked scallops and then the basil leaves.

Garganelli con Salmone e Gamberi Garganelli with Salmon and Shrimp   serves 4

12 ounces salmon fillets

¾ cup plus 2 tablespoons dry white wine

a few basil leaves, plus extra for garnish

sea salt and freshly ground black pepper

⅔ cup heavy cream

6 ripe plum tomatoes, peeled and finely chopped

12 ounces garganelli (see page 138)

4 ounces shelled cooked shrimp

1 Put the salmon in a wide, shallow pan, skin side up. Pour the wine over, scatter in the basil, and sprinkle with salt and pepper. Bring to a boil, cover, reduce the heat, and simmer no more than 5 minutes. Using a pancake turner, lift the fish out; set aside to cool slightly.

2 Add the cream and tomatoes to the liquid remaining in the pan and bring to a boil. Stir well, lower the heat, and simmer, uncovered, 10 to 15 minutes, until the sauce thickens slightly.

3 Meanwhile, cook the pasta in a large pot of boiling salted water until al dente, or just tender but still firm to the bite.

4 When cool enough to handle, flake the fish into large chunks, discarding the skin and any bones. Add the fish to the sauce, together with the shrimp, shaking the pan until the fish and shellfish are coated. Taste and adjust the seasoning.

5 Drain the pasta and transfer it to a warm serving bowl. Spoon the sauce over the pasta and toss well to combine. Serve immediately, garnished with more basil leaves.

Variations

Instead of the salmon use any firm white fish, such as cod or haddock, or lobster meat left over from the recipe on page 144. I have cooked this using sea bass, and it was very delicious.

Tagliolini Neri con Vongole e Cozze Squid Ink Tagliolini with Clams and Mussels
serves 6 as an appetizer, 4 as a main course

Served in a white china bowl, this makes a stunning dish for a dinner party.

I pound fresh mussels
I pound fresh clams
4 tablespoons olive oil
I small onion, finely chopped
2 garlic cloves, finely chopped
large handful fresh flat-leaf parsley, plus extra to garnish
sea salt and freshly ground black pepper
¾ cup dry white wine
I cup fish stock
I small fresh red chile, seeded and chopped
12 ounces tagliolini or tagliarini (page 133) nero (squid ink pasta; pages 8 to 12)

1 Scrub the mussels and clams under cold water and discard any that are damaged or that are open and do not close when sharply tapped against the countertop.

2 Heat the half of the oil in a large saucepan over medium heat. Add the onion and cook slowly about 5 minutes, until soft. Sprinkle in the garlic, about half the parsley, and salt and pepper to taste. Add the mussels and clams and pour in the wine. Cover and bring to a boil over high heat. Cook about 5 minutes, shaking the pan frequently, until the shellfish have opened.

3 Transfer the mussels and clams to a fine strainer set over a bowl and let the liquid drain through. Discard the aromatics in the strainer, together with any mussels or clams that have failed to open. Rinse out the pan. Return the liquid to the clean pan and add the fish stock. Finely chop the remaining parsley and add it to the liquid, along with the minced chile. Bring to a boil, then lower the heat and simmer, stirring, for a few minutes, until slightly reduced. Turn off the heat.

4 Remove and discard the top shells of about half the mussels and clams, reserving any juices. Put all the mussels and clams with their juices in the pan of liquid and season with salt and pepper, then cover the pan tightly and set aside.

5 Cook the pasta in a large pot of boiling salted water until al dente, or just tender but still firm to the bite.

6 Drain the pasta well, then return it to the pot and toss it with the remaining oil. Return the pan of shellfish to high heat, toss to heat through quickly, and combine with the liquid and seasonings.

7 Divide the pasta among 4 to 6 warm plates. Spoon the shellfish mixture over and then serve immediately, sprinkled with more parsley.

Strangozzi ai Fiori di Zucca con Pollo Strangozzi with Zucchini Flowers and Chicken serves 4

Strangozzi are a slightly smaller version of strozzapreti or "priest stranglers," a special kind of short pasta shape from Modena. You can buy packages of them in Italian delicatessens or use gemelli, a similar kind of twisted pasta.

2 skinless and boneless chicken breast halves, 12 ounces total
sea salt and freshly ground black pepper
4 tablespoons unsalted butter
2 tablespoons olive oil
1 small onion, thinly sliced
1½ cups small zucchini cut into thin julienne strips
1 garlic clove, crushed
2 teaspoons finely chopped fresh marjoram
12 ounces dried strangozzi (see above)
large handful zucchini flowers, thoroughly washed and dried
thinly shaved Parmesan cheese, to garnish

1 Season the chicken with salt and pepper and broil under medium heat, turning once, 25 minutes, until golden. Cut into even-size pieces and set side.

2 Heat the butter and half of the oil in a medium-size saucepan. Add the onion and sauté about 5 minutes, until soft. Add the zucchini to the pan and add the garlic, marjoram, and salt and pepper to taste. Add the chicken pieces and cook 8 minutes, until the zucchini are colored.

3 Meanwhile, cook the pasta in a large pot of boiling salted water until al dente, or just tender but still firm to the bite.

4 Set aside a few whole zucchini flowers for garnish, then roughly shred the rest and stir them into the zucchini mixture. Taste and adjust the seasoning.

5 Drain the pasta, transfer it to a large warm bowl, and add the remaining oil. Toss, add the zucchini mixture, and toss again. Top with Parmesan shavings and the reserved zucchini flowers. Serve immediately.

Vincisgrassi Aperto Open Lasagne with Fresh Porcini and Prosciutto serves 4 to 6

Vincisgrassi is an extravagant version of lasagne from the Marche, traditionally featuring brains, sweetbreads, and chicken livers. Its name is said to come from an Austrian general, Windisch Graetz, for whom it was created.

½ recipe egg pasta dough (page 8)

sea salt and freshly ground black pepper

14 ounces fresh porcini mushrooms, sliced

4 tablespoons extra-virgin olive oil

7 ounces prosciutto, cut into julienne strips

1 cup light cream

3 tablespoons chopped fresh flat-leaf parsley

1¼ cups freshly grated Parmesan cheese

white truffle oil or, if possible, a little shaved white truffle

FOR THE BESCIAMELLA SAUCE

⅝ cup (1¼ sticks) unsalted butter

⅓ cup flour, preferably Italian 00-grade

1¼ quarts milk, heated

1 Roll the dough through the pasta machine as you would for lasagne. Cut the pasta pieces into 5-inch squares. Cook the squares, a few at a time, in a large pot of boiling salted water. Drain and place on clean dish towels. Set aside.

2 Make the besciamella sauce: Melt 4 tablespoons of the butter, add the flour, and blend in well. Add the hot milk, a little at a time, whisking well after each addition. Set aside.

3 Cook the porcini in the oil until soft and add to the besciamella sauce. Stir in the prosciutto, cream, and parsley. Season with salt and pepper and bring to a boil; remove the pan from the heat.

4 Heat the oven to 425°F. To assemble the vincisgrassi, butter a gratin dish (or individual gratin dishes) and cover the bottom with a layer of pasta. Then spread over a layer of besciamella, dot with butter, and sprinkle with Parmesan. Continue making layer after layer, finishing with a besciamella layer and a sprinkling of Parmesan. Bake for 20 minutes, until bubbling. Finish under a hot broiler, if necessary, to give the top a good color.

5 Serve with a drizzle of truffle oil or, best of all, shavings of white truffle, and a little more Parmesan cheese.

Pastiera Napoletana Neapolitan Ricotta Tart   serves 10

I thought I ought to have at least one sweet pasta dish. There are many variations of this famous and rich classical dish from the Cappuccino Convent in Amalfi. I think it's best eaten the day after it is made.

FOR THE PASTRY DOUGH
1 cup (2 sticks) unsalted butter
¾ cup plus 2 tablespoons superfine sugar
4 egg yolks
3 cups Italian 00-grade flour, plus more for dusting

FOR THE FILLING
2 cups ricotta
½ cup plus 2 tablespoons superfine sugar
1 teaspoon ground cinnamon
grated zest and juice of 1 unwaxed lemon
4 tablespoons orange-flower water
4 ounces candied orange or mixed peel
1 egg, separated
1¼ cups milk
6 ounces vermicelli
large pinch salt
confectioners' sugar for dusting

1 Make the pastry dough: Put the butter and sugar in a bowl and cream together. Add the egg yolks and then gradually add the flour, mixing well to make a soft dough. Wrap in waxed paper and chill in the refrigerator 30 minutes.

2 Heat the oven to 375°F. Make the filling: Put the ricotta, all but 2 tablespoons of the sugar, the cinnamon, half the lemon zest, the lemon juice, the orange-flower water, candied peel, and the egg yolk in a bowl and beat together.

3 In a small saucepan, bring the milk to a boil. Add the vermicelli, the remaining sugar and lemon zest and the salt and simmer until the vermicelli absorbs nearly all the milk.

4 While it is still warm, stir the pasta carefully into the ricotta mixture. Whisk the egg white until it just holds its shape, then fold it into the mixture.

5 On a lightly floured surface, roll out the dough and use two-thirds of it to line an 11-inch loose-bottom tart pan: It is a very delicate dough, so it may tear readily, but you can patch it very easily.

6 Fill the pastry with the ricotta mixture, then cut the remaining dough into ¼-inch strips and arrange it in a lattice pattern over the top of the tart.

7 Bake for 40 to 50 minutes, until golden. Dust with confectioners' sugar; serve warm or cold.

index

agnolotti con Taleggio e maggiorana, 132

agnolotti with Taleggio and
marjoram, 132

Alfredo's fettuccine, 40

anchovies:
anchovies, capers, and tomatoes, 72
orecchiette with broccoli and, 102
spaghetti with olives and, 69

artichokes, penne with shrimp and, 101

arugula, 112
orecchiette with, 95

asparagus, 112
garganelli with cream and, 138

beans:
minestrone with, 22
pasta, bean, and vegetable soup, 24

beef:
Bolognese sauce, 134
lasagne with meatballs, 129

Bolognese sauce, 134

bonbons con funghi di bosco e ricotta, 140

brandelli con melanzane e zucchini, 62

brandelli with eggplant and
zucchini sauce, 62

broccoli:
macaroni with cauliflower and, 68
orecchiette with anchovies and, 102
pasta with, 92
stuffed giant pasta shells, 63

bucatini:
with zucchini, 40
with sardines and fennel, 103
with sausage and pancetta, 78

bucatini alla posillipo, 78

bucatini alle sarde e finocchio, 103

bucatini con zucchini, 40

buckwheat pasta, 60

cabbage, pasta layer with beans,
potatoes, and, 60

cannelloni:
with fava beans and ricotta, 114
with saffron sauce, 139

cannelloni alla zafferano, 139

cannelloni con fave e ricotta, 114

cappellacci alla Bolognese, 134

cappellacci with Bolognese sauce, 134

cauliflower, macaroni with broccoli
and, 68

cheese:
agnolotti with Taleggio and
marjoram, 132
baby spinach and blue cheese, 96
bonbons filled with wild
mushrooms and ricotta, 140
bucatini with zucchini, 40
cannelloni with fava beans and
ricotta, 114
cannelloni with saffron sauce, 139
cheese cappellacci with Bolognese
sauce, 34
farfalle with Gorgonzola cream, 45
four cheeses (stir-in sauce), 46
fried ravioli, 118
Neapolitan ricotta tart, 156
pansotti with herbs and, 116
penne with fava beans and ricotta, 39
prosciutto and Gruyère cheese, 46
pumpkin, sage, and ricotta, 145
rigatoni with Gorgonzola and pine
nuts, 41
Sardinian ravioli, 117
spaghetti with pepper and, 34
spinach and ricotta, 145
spinach, ricotta, and tomato pasta
roll, 137
tortellini with butter and sage, 121
tortellini with ricotta, 109
walnut, ricotta, and basil, 145

chestnuts, spaghetti with sage and, 90

chiaroscuro, 149

chicken:
farfalle with cherry tomatoes and, 74
penne with broccoli, cheese, and, 76
strangozzi with zucchini flowers
and, 153

chicken livers, pasta soup with peas
and, 31

chickpeas:
fettuccine with, 48
minestrone with pasta and, 19

chiles: pasta Vesuvius, 90

chitarra con sardine e pane grattati, 69

chitarra with sardines and bread
crumbs, 69

clams:
clam and pasta soup, 29
linguine with turnip greens and, 98
squid ink tagliolini with mussels
and, 151

cod: Sardinian fish stew, 26

conchiglie, 13
minestrone with pasta and
chickpeas, 19
pasta pie with squid and peas, 105
with fennel and tomato sauce, 89
with roasted vegetables, 64

*conchiglie con salsa di finocchio e
pomodoro,* 89

conchiglie con salsa di noci e funghi, 42

conchiglie con verdure arrostite, 64

conchiglie grandi farcite, 63

cooking pasta, 14–15

crab, ravioli with, 143

culurjones, 117

ditali: pasta with broccoli, 92

dried pasta, cooking, 14

egg pasta, 8, 13

eggplant, 96
brandelli with eggplant and
zucchini sauce, 62
penne with eggplant sauce, 87

eliche con salsiccia e radicchio, 77

eliche with sausage and radicchio, 77

farfalle, 13
with chicken and cherry
tomatoes, 74
with Gorgonzola cream, 45

farfalle alla crema di Gorgonzola, 45

farfalle con pollo e pomodorini, 74

farmhouse soup, 25

fava beans:
fava beans, red onions, mint, and
Pecorino, 72
cannelloni with ricotta and, 114
penne with ricotta and, 39

fennel and tomato sauce, conchiglie
with, 89

fettuccine:
Alfredo's, 40

pasta Vesuvius, 90
with chickpeas, 48

fettuccine all'Alfredo, 40

fettuccine con ceci, 48

fresh pasta, cooking, 14, 15

fusilli, 13

garganelli:
with asparagus and cream, 138
with salmon and shrimp, 150
with spring vegetables, 87

garganelli con asparagi e panna, 138

garganelli con salmone e gamberi, 150

garganelli con verdure di stagione, 87

garlic:
pasta with oil and, 34
rigatoni with roasted garlic, chile,
and mushrooms, 67

Genoese minestrone, 18

ham: vermicelli with saffron, 50

herbs: seven deadly sins, 96

lasagne, 11
lasagne Bolognese, 127
open lasagne with fresh porcini and
Parma ham, 154
with meatballs, 129

lasagne alla Bolognese, 127

lasagne con polpettini, 129

lemons, mint and, 112

lentil and pasta soup, 25

linguine con vongole e cime di rape, 98

linguine with clams and turnip greens, 98

lobster and herbs, 144

macaroni:
farmhouse soup, 25
with broccoli and cauliflower, 68
with dried tuna roe, 54–5

maccheroni, 13

maccheroni alla bottarga di favignana,
54–5

maccheroni con broccoli in tegame, 68

mandilli di seta con pesto, 108

meat broth, pasta in, 31

millescosedde, 24

minestra con pasta e verdure arrostite, 21

minestrone:
  with autumn/winter vegetables, 22
  with beans, 22
  with pasta and chickpeas, 19
  with pasta and roasted vegetables, 21
  with spring vegetables, 22
  with summer vegetables, 23
minestrone alla Genovese, 18
minestrone di fagioli, 22
minestrone di pasta e ceci, 19
minestrone estate, 23
minestrone inverno, 22
minestrone primavera, 22
mint and lemons, 112
mushrooms:
  bonbons filled with wild mushrooms
    and ricotta, 140
  open lasagne with fresh porcini and
    Parma ham, 154
  pasta shells with walnut and
    mushroom sauce, 44
  rigatoni with roasted garlic, chile
    and, 67
  spaghetti with, 59
  spaghetti with pancetta, tuna,
    and, 53
mussels, squid ink tagliolini with clams
  and, 151

Neapolitan ricotta tart, 156
noodles, 11

olive oil, 13
orecchiette:
  with anchovies and broccoli, 102
  with arugula, 95
orecchiette con acciughe e broccoli, 102
orecchiette con rucola, 95

packets, cooking pasta in, 71–3
pansotti con erbe e formaggi, 116
pansotti with herbs and cheese, 116
pappardelle, 13
  pasta and peas, 58
  with rabbit sauce, 123
  with truffles and porcini, 133
pappardelle con sugo di coniglio, 123
pappardelle con tartufi e porcini, 133
Parma ham, open lasagne with fresh
  porcini and, 154
parsley, 112
pasta al cartoccio con tonno, pomodoro

e patate, 71
pasta alla crudaiola, 35
pasta all'aglio e olio, 34
pasta con calabrese, 92
pasta con piselli, 58
pasta con spinaci, 12
pasta con sugo di verdure, 58
pasta machines, 11
pasta nero, 12
pasta pie with squid and peas, 105
pasta shapes:
  lentil and pasta soup, 25
  pasta, bean, and vegetable soup, 24
pasta shells:
  stuffed giant pasta shells, 63
  with walnut and mushroom
    sauce, 44
pasta verde, 12
pasta Vesuvio, 90
pasticciata con calamari e piselli, 105
pastiera Napoletana, 156
pastina in brodo, 31
pastina in brodo con piselli e fegatini, 31
peas:
  green tagliatelle with fresh pea
    sauce, 81
  pasta and peas, 58
  pasta pie with squid and, 105
  pasta soup with chicken livers
    and, 31
penne, 13
  roasted red pepper pesto with
    penne rigate, 111
  with chicken, broccoli, and
    cheese, 76
  with eggplant sauce, 87
  with fava beans and ricotta, 39
  with gratinéed tomatoes, 86
  with shrimp and artichokes, 101
penne ai gamberi e carciofi, 101
penne alla rusticana, 76
penne con fave e ricotta, 39
penne con pomodori gratinati, 86
penne con salsa di melanzane, 87
peppers:
  minestrone with summer
    vegetables, 23
  roasted red pepper pesto with
    penne rigate, 111
pesce con fregula, 26
pesto:
  Genoese minestrone, 18

roasted red pepper pesto with
  penne rigate, 111
squares of pasta with, 108
trenette with green beans,
  potatoes and, 91
*pesto di peperoni arrostiti con penne
  rigate,* 111
pizzocheri della Valtellina, 60
pork:
  Bolognese sauce, 134
  lasagne with meatballs, 129
  ravioli with turkey and, 126
portion sizes, 15
potatoes:
  pasta layer with cabbage, beans,
    and, 60
  pasta in paper with tuna,
    tomatoes and, 71
  Sardinian ravioli, 117
  trenette with pesto, green beans,
    and, 91
prosciutto and Gruyère cheese, 46
pumpkin, sage, and ricotta, 145

rabbit sauce, pappardelle with, 123
radicchio, tagliatelle with cream
  and, 138
ravioli, 11
  fried ravioli, 118
  Sardinian ravioli, 117
  with crab, 143
  with pork and turkey, 126
ravioli al granchio, 143
ravioli alla Romagnola, 126
ravioli fritti, 118
red snapper: Sardinian fish stew, 26
rigatoni, 13
  country-style, 65
  with Gorgonzola and pine nuts, 41
  with roasted garlic, chile, and
    mushrooms, 67
rigatoni casalinga, 65
*rigatoni con aglio arrostito, peperoncino
  e funghi,* 67
rigatoni con pignoli e Gorgonzola, 41
rotolo ripieno, 137

saffron:
  cannelloni with, 139
  vermicelli with, 50
sage, tortellini with butter and, 121
salmon, garganelli with shrimp and, 150

sardines:
  bucatini with fennel and, 103
  chitarra with breadcrumbs and, 69
Sardinian fish stew, 26
Sardinian ravioli, 117
sauces, matching to pasta shapes, 13
sausage:
  bucatini with pancetta and, 78
  eliche with radicchio and, 77
scallops:
  squid ink pasta with ricotta and, 149
  tagliatelle with, 146
serving pasta, 15
seven deadly sins, 96
shrimp, 46
  garganelli with salmon and, 150
  penne with artichokes and, 101
soups, 17–31
spaghetti, 13, 14
  pasta in paper with tuna,
    tomatoes, and potatoes, 71
  pasta with garlic and oil, 34
  with anchovies and olives, 69
  with cheese and pepper, 34
  with chestnuts and sage, 90
  with fresh tomato sauce, 35
  with mushrooms, 59
  with mushrooms, pancetta, and
    tuna, 53
  with puréed tomatoes, bell pepper,
    basil, and mint, 37
  with tiny tomatoes, 84
  with tomatoes and pancetta, 49
  with veal meatballs, 124
spaghetti al mortaio, 37
spaghetti alla Bellini, 59
spaghetti alla carrettiera, 53
spaghetti alla rancetto, 49
spaghetti alla Siracusana, 69
spaghetti con cacio e pepe, 34
spaghetti con castagne e salvia, 90
spaghetti con polpettini di vitello, 124
spaghetti con pomodori freschi, 35
spaghetti con pomodorini, 84
spaghettini, 13
spinach:
  baby spinach and blue cheese, 96
  pasta con spinaci, 12
  pasta verde, 12
  spinach and ricotta, 145
  spinach and tomatoes, 46
  spinach, ricotta, and tomato pasta

roll, 137
squares of pasta with pesto, 108
squid, pasta pie with peas and, 105
squid ink:
    pasta nero, 12
    squid ink pasta with ricotta and
        scallops, 149
    squid ink tagliolini with clams and
        mussels, 151
strangozzi ai fiori di zucca con pollo, 153
strangozzi with zucchini flowers and
    chicken, 153
stuffed pasta shapes, cooking, 14

tagliarini al tartufo bianco, 133
tagliarini with white truffle, 133
tagliatelle, 13
    green tagliatelle with fresh pea
        sauce, 81
    with radicchio and cream, 138
    with scallops, 146
tagliatelle con capesanti, 146
tagliatelle con radicchio e panna, 138
tagliatelle verdi al sugo di piselli, 81
tagliolini, 13
    squid ink tagliolini with clams and
        mussels, 151
tagliolini neri con vongole e cozze, 151
tart, Neapolitan ricotta, 156
tomatoes:
    pasta in paper with tuna,
        potatoes, and, 71
    pasta with raw tomato sauce, 35
    penne with gratinéed tomatoes, 86
    spaghetti with fresh tomato sauce, 35
    spaghetti with puréed tomatoes,
        bell pepper, basil, and mint, 37
    spaghetti with tiny tomatoes, 84
    spaghetti with pancetta and, 49
    spinach and, 46
    sun-dried tomatoes and radicchio, 96
    tomatoes, olives, parsley, and
        garlic, 72
tortellini:
    with butter and sage, 121
    with ricotta, 109
tortellini con burro e salvia, 121
tortellini con ricotta, 109
trenette alla Genovese, 91

trenette with pesto, green beans,
    and potatoes, 91
truffles:
    pappardelle with porcini and, 133
    tagliarini with white truffle, 133
tuna:
    pasta in paper with tomatoes,
        potatoes, and, 71
    spaghetti with mushrooms,
        pancetta, and, 53
tuna roe, macaroni with, 54–5
turkey, ravioli with pork and, 126
turnip greens, linguine with clams and,
    98

veal meatballs, spaghetti with, 124
vegetables:
    conchiglie with roasted vegetables, 64
    garganelli with spring vegetables, 87
    minestrone with autumn/winter
        vegetables, 22
    minestrone with pasta and roasted
        vegetables, 21
    minestrone with spring vegetables, 22
    minestrone with summer
        vegetables, 23
    pasta with green vegetable sauce, 58
vermicelli, 13
    Genoese minestrone, 18
    minestrone with pasta and roasted
        vegetables, 21
    with saffron, 50
vermicelli allo zafferano, 50
vincisgrassi aperto, 154

walnuts:
    pasta shells with walnut and
        mushroom sauce, 44
    walnut, ricotta, and basil, 145

zucchini flowers, 72
    strangozzi with chicken and, 153
zucchini, 72
    bucatini with, 40
zuppa casalinga, 25
zuppa di lenticchie e pastina, 25
zuppa di vongole e pastina, 29

author's acknowledgments

The team of professionals behind the making of this book have been superb. Firstly, **Jane O'Shea** for commissioning me, being so consistently enthusiastic on the subject and for her constant gentle reassurance.

Lewis Esson, editor extraordinaire, for being so professional, for anticipating so much, and for loving the food so much.

Mary Evans, the art director, for her dedication and for her eye for excellence, which is quite inspirational. Thank you for soldiering on with this project.

Pippa Cuthbert, my friend and assistant on the food styling. Thank you for your calmness, constant smiles, and willingness to run out to the shops yet again. You have a sparkling career ahead of you.

Linda Tubby for her fabulous food styling.

Kate O'Donnel, my friend and my typist, for deciphering my scribble with such great humor, professionalism, and dedication.

Pete Cassidy, the photographer, such a joy to work with, you are the very best in the world, your work stands out from the crowd.

Kate Whitaker for her quiet efficiency and anticipation of all our needs.

Books for Cooks for their friendship, support, advice, and regular work. Thank you so much, **Rosie and Eric,** I do so enjoy being part of the team.

Food styling **Ursula Ferrigno assisted by Pippa Cuthbert, except for pages 28, 52, 75, 80, 100, 125, 128, 135, 146, 150, 155 by Linda Tubby**

Publishing director **Jane O'Shea**
Art director **Mary Evans**
Editor & project manager **Lewis Esson**
Photography **Peter Cassidy assisted by Kate Whitaker**
Styling **Roísín Neild**
Production **Tracy Hart**